CHRISTIANITY
AND THE OCCULT

J. Stafford Wright

SCRIPTURE UNION
5 Wigmore Street
London W1H OAD

Other books and booklets by J. Stafford Wright:

WHAT IS MAN?

SOME MODERN RELIGIONS *(with J. Oswald Sanders)*

SPIRITUALISM

ZEN AND THE CHRISTIAN

EZRA—JOB (Bible Study Books)

LAMENTATIONS—DANIEL (Bible Study Books)

ISBN 0 85421 299 X

Biblical quotations are from the Revised Standard Version, unless otherwise stated.

Printed by A. McLay & Co. Ltd. Cardiff and London

CONTENTS

PREFACE

This book is not anecdotal, although it contains some true stories. Nor is it a string of Bible passages intended to close discussion. Rather, it asks two questions. First: How can psychic experiences be related to what I experience in space-time? This means trying to map out our inner world of experience, about which we know rather less than we know about outer space. Secondly: How can psychic experiences be assessed in the light of the Bible, which as Christians we use as our guidebook? It is true that the Bible was not given to teach us science or psychology or the findings of psychical research, but its teachings, if they are valid, must be capable of positive interpretation in the light of every true discovery in every age.

So this book will call for some hard thinking. But I have tried not to make it technical. When tempted to use a difficult word, I have tried to rethink what I wanted to say so that anyone could grasp the argument. At the same time I hope that any readers who already have a fair knowledge of the literature of psychical research, will be able to read between the lines, and make their own additions.

I was helped by all those who responded to the appeal by the Scripture Union, and sent in reports of personal experiences, even though I could use only a limited number.

Two letters warned against the publication of such a book as this, on the grounds that publicity is likely to arouse interest in the subject and induce readers to try occultism for themselves. Unfortunately the idea of 'having a go' is already too widespread, even among Christians. However, this book does avoid detailed practical descriptions and we hope that it will provide no such encouragement.

I do not want to be type-cast as an expert on the occult. The sphere of the psychic is, after all, only one small part of human experience, the range of which, in realms both human and divine, is so wonderful that life will not be long enough to explore it all and see how the parts fit together. And I am convinced that we cannot in any case fit them together rightly unless we keep a close hold on what God has shown us in the Bible. The Bible does not contract our thinking, but keeps opening up fresh clues to truth. This conviction I have worked out positively in *What is Man?* (Paternoster Press), *Spiritualism* (Church Bookroom booklet), *Zen and the Christian* (SPCK booklet) and in an up-to-date revision of a remarkable book by Dr. A. T. Schofield, *Christian Sanity* (Oliphants).

Finally, I am very grateful to unknown readers of my original script for their most helpful suggestions, and to Mrs. Yvonne Odjidja for turning my handwriting into typescript without having to leave more than a couple of blanks.

J. Stafford Wright

Bristol, 1971.

INTRODUCTION

WHY THE HUNGER FOR THE OCCULT?

by Anne C. Long, Lecturer in Religious Education, Gipsy Hill College of Education.

Interest in the supernatural is no new thing. In Old Testament times the Egyptians had their magicians, the Babylonians their astrologers and the Assyrians their dream manuals: perhaps not a far cry from our women's magazines with 'Your Fate in the Stars', our horoscope almanacs, fortune-tellers and charm bracelets. Is it simply a case of 'these things always have been and ever shall be', and the less said about them the better if we want to avoid trouble? If that is our attitude, the growing appetite for the psychic, occult and demonic that we see in Western culture today will be something which we, as Christians, will be unprepared for.

Even if we have not yet been confronted personally with these issues, we need not search far to discover them. There is a growing number of horoscope magazines in the local newsagent's or bookseller's, as well as the popular *Man, Myth and Magic* which attained a circulation of about a quarter of a million at 4/- a week. Until recently many shops sold Ouija boards without restraint, with printed instructions as to how to contact spirits. Many schoolchildren and young people have experimented with this and other glass-moving games.

In recent discussion with a group of non-Christian students I discovered that most had, at school or college, joined in such games out of curiosity and several had withdrawn frightened at what had happened. Every student in that group believed in the reality of a supernatural realm, though none claimed a personal relationship with God. Twenty years ago this would not have been so.

Areas of the occult are also being exploited by the film industry. One film, *Rosemary's Baby*, was a deliberate parody of the Incarnation in which Rosemary conceived a baby by Satan. On a smaller but no less influential scale, T.V. seems to be introducing a growing number of documentaries and discussions about magic and the occult.

Some might feel 'this is all an inevitable part of the cultural rat-race and, as long as we avoid the ominous rat and maintain our faith, all will be well'. But rats multiply unless destroyed and maybe a policy of avoidance cannot go on indefinitely. Those of us working and living with young people know very well that this whole area of the supernatural has become established in our present culture and is fast increasing in influence and variety. How would *you* advise a young person in whose eyes mysticism and occultism are legitimate and desirable pursuits? A drop-out fellow recently said, 'Western society is too materialistic, and many young people are looking for something new.' Are youth leaders prepared to take up such comments seriously?

At a Christian houseparty for young people someone suggested holding a seance but at the very mention of the word one boy, who had previously joined in a seance 'for fun', was violently attacked by an evil spirit, which the camp officer had to be called in to deal with. Are Christian camp staff prepared for similar invasions? Two students I know, asked to prepare a topic of their own choice, selected magic, attempted correspondence with a witch and attended a witches' shop in London. What is my responsibility in this? Are teachers prepared to get involved in the fringe activities of those they teach or offer valid reasons for their non-involvement? These are pressing questions today. The Bible does not recommend us to dabble in these things ourselves, but it does offer authoritative teaching on God, man, Satan and the supernatural that it is imperative for us to understand.

In an age when we are exposed to a more dazzling patchwork of thinking than ever before, there seem to be four possible attitudes that can be held by Christians regarding the occult. Firstly, that these influences in our contemporary culture are inevitable and here to stay, and that there is nothing to worry about. Secondly, that there is everything to worry about, so we should shut our eyes and ears, bury our heads—and, probably, communicate nothing. Thirdly, that it is all highly intriguing and we should learn as much as possible, even by having a little dabble ourselves. Fourthly, that these things are likely to increase, must be taken seriously and are part of Satan's desperate attempt to invalidate Christ's victory. If this last assumption is true, intelligence about the facts is not enough—it will rather be a case of intelligence plus caution, plus, above all, spiritual weapons for a spiritual battle.

Much as we may find this resurgence of interest in the occult regrettable or alarming, we should not be surprised. It is the logical outcome of thinking that has dispensed with God. The majority of modern young people have no time for God; yet, because they were made by Him, they cannot help fumbling for meaning and significance beyond their materialistic environment in the direction of the supernatural. What lies behind this paradox?

At one stage in history God was generally accepted as Creator and Controller of the Universe. He had made and peopled it and the moral absolutes governing it found their reference point in Himself. Thus the concept of 'good' was related to a 'good' God, and evil was the antithesis of it. Likewise the concept of 'right' was anchored in God's own nature, and 'wrong' was its antithesis. With this fixed reference point people knew what was meant when someone said, 'Be a good girl' or 'Stealing is wrong'. At the risk of over-simplification we could represent it visually like this:

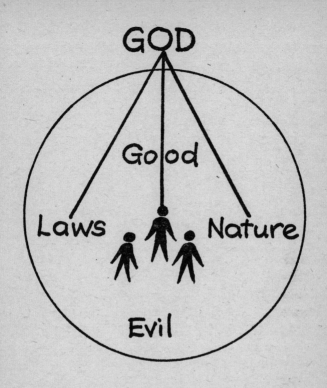

But with the onset of Humanism philosophers began to think differently: they rejected the idea of a governing Creator God. So now man made his own codes of morality within a closed system. Because the fixed point of reference had gone, standards became relative according to men's opinions. 'Good' and 'evil' were no longer absolute but became accommodated to men's social needs and estimates. Man was now his own authority.

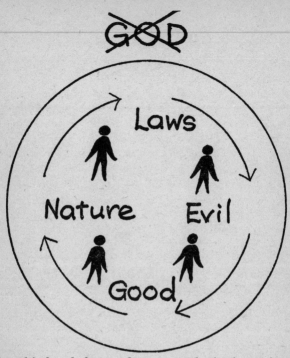

But this has led too often to synthetic, inconsistent norms which fail to satisfy. We are now faced with great unrest and protest. Many young people are wanting to overthrow the codes of living offered by their seniors. To them a closed system abounding in inconsistencies is intolerable and, whilst still rejecting God-talk, they are seeking to penetrate the boundaries of experience in a new quest for reality in supernatural realms. Through mysticism, drugs and magic many are seeking some authentic experience which will act as a relief from the frustration of thinking.

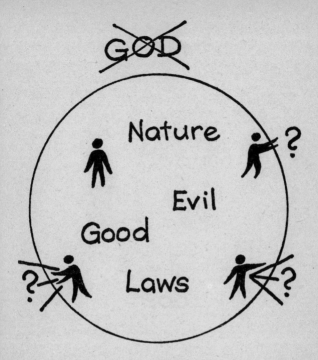

If we are to understand the new emphasis on the occult in contemporary culture it is vital that we understand what has happened to men's thinking about God and the universe through the ages. To regard it as a random phenomenon is misleading and inaccurate. It is the logical outcome of dispensing with God. The trend is likely to persist rather than cease and, if we are to approach the younger generation seriously and intelligently, we must also approach their thinking and culture seriously, both on an intellectual and a spiritual plane. We must recognize the activities of Satan, understand what the Bible teaches and affirm the certain victory of Jesus Christ.

It is our contemporary situation that makes books like this not a curiosity but a necessity.

1. WHEN CHRISTIANS CANNOT BE NEUTRAL

WHEN you opened this book, you might have been rather daunted by the sight of several chapters before you come to the occult. There is a good reason for this arrangement.

This is not a book of anecdotes and snap answers. To deal with the subject properly, one must have a background against which to interpret phenomena. Consider the following illustration. One night you wake up and see the form of a friend who is living hundreds of miles away. He appears to be dressed in dripping wet clothes. He looks at you, smiles, and vanishes. Next day you hear that, at about the time you apparently saw him, your friend was accidentally drowned.

So it was a ghost, and you will no doubt talk about it as a ghost story. But, if you want it to be more than a story, you are bound to look at the events against quite an extensive background, and to ask various questions. For example: what is the nature of vision, when I can see something with my eyes which is not physically there? This alone involves the whole question of hallucinations and their causes. If it was my friend's spirit, what about his clothes—were they spirit clothes too? Was he actually transported to my room, or did I see him by some form of telepathy? If the latter, did he create the telepathic vision, or did I? If it was actually my friend, what does *actually* mean, since obviously he was not as I knew him in the body? Or did I imagine the whole thing as a kind of waking dream? What evidence is there that someone with a distant friend will every so often express his fears for his safety in an anxiety dream? If he had already died when he appeared to me, ought I to try from my side to make contact with him again through a seance of some kind? Where is he now?

Before we can begin to think sensibly about questions like these we need a consistent and reliable background against which to seek an interpretation of happenings like these; happenings which the physical sciences cannot explain.

Let us now begin to set the scene, and show how a Christian is to make a proper judgement.

* * * * * *

There are plenty of things in life that anyone can use and enjoy. There are some things, such as brain surgery, that can safely be handled only by someone who is prepared to go through extensive training. There are a few things, such as heroin injection, that it is both most unwise and most dangerous for anyone to touch at all. Into which category do we place the occult?

If this book simply aimed to establish whether dabbling in the occult is wise or dangerous to humanity, there would be little, once that had been settled, to discuss. Even without acknowledging God, sensible human beings try to do what is wise and avoid what is destructive to individuals and society.

So, if plunging into the occult is wise, we can all enjoy it if we wish; if it is destructive, neither Christians nor non-Christians ought to touch it. If that were all, it would be enough to work out this book on experimental grounds only.

But for the Christian there are criteria beyond *wise* and *destructive;* namely *right* and *wrong.* Humanists may also use these terms, but, while they use them to describe what is expedient or inexpedient, the Christian sees them as related also to God and as eternal realities. The Christian holds that true humanity and true Christianity are the same, and that the revealed will of God comes to make man fully human. He holds also that in the person of Jesus Christ, and in the Bible, we have God's revelation of Himself and of His relationship with man. To be in a right relationship with God is to be *good* (and will result in *wisdom* humanly speaking); to be in a wrong relationship with God is to commit *sin* (and this will result in *destructiveness* humanly speaking).

Once we introduce the Bible as God's Word to man, the veil is partly lifted on the unseen and eternal world, since God's purpose is not simply to lay down moral commands but to unfold the way of union with Himself. He shows us that we are not the only intelligent inhabitants of this universe, but that there are unseen beings, both on His side and against Him. As we study the whole Bible, we find that separate pieces of information can be brought together into a coherent and meaningful whole.

If a scientist can make an assessment of psychical research in the light of the physical sciences, or a philosopher in the light of philosophical concepts, a Christian may make his assessment in the light of what his Book says about God and man and other beings. And we may be sure that, if God has revealed anything in the Bible, it can be shown to make sense in thought and experience.

As we shall be trying to make a Christian assessment, it is worth taking a little space for assessing Christianity itself. Probably most readers of this book have a fair idea of what a Christian is, but anyone with an inadequate knowledge of what the Christian faith involves could easily misunderstand some of the points we shall be making.

A Christian is commonly thought of as someone with reasonable standards, someone who is no worse than his neighbour. This is a compliment to the Christian faith as it has come to us down the ages. In Old Testament times the prophets had great difficulty in persuading the people that religion need trouble about morality (e.g. Isa. 1 and Jer. 7). Today we commonly find people unconvinced that morality needs any link with religion. Christians agree that behaviour is intimately bound up with their faith, but New Testament Christianity, which is rooted in Christ, involves a good deal more than morality. Indeed the history of the Christian Church from its earliest days shows that it was the new revelation about God that transformed men's attitude towards moral issues.

The New Testament revelation sets Christianity apart from all other world religions. The founders of all other religions produced sets of teachings which might equally well have been produced by any other enlightened men. Jesus Christ not only produced teachings on human behaviour, but He presented Himself as divine in a unique sense, and as God-Man He did what no mere man could do. In choosing to die on the Cross, Himself sinless, He gave Himself as a sacrifice in order to take away sin in a way that a word of simple forgiveness could not do. Then He rose again from the dead—not simply surviving death, but with His body made alive and transformed. With this body He returned to His Father, and then poured out His Spirit to infuse His victorious power into His people.

There is one further point of significance. The founder of no other religion was expected to come as Jesus Christ was. The Old Testament had prepared the Jewish nation for their Messiah. There were differences of opinion as to what would be the nature of His life, but the early Christians found that the various predictive strands in the Old Testament met in Jesus Christ, in Whom was seen deity and humanity, suffering and glory.

It may sound easy to evade the issue altogether by saying, "The Churches are so divided that it is impossible to declare that the Bible expressly teaches this or that". But consider where the divisions come. During the first four centuries Christian thinkers thrashed out what the Bible says about God and the Person of Jesus Christ. They treated the Bible as the scientist treats the universe, recognizing that all sorts of phenomena exist, but believing that these can be brought together under useful formulae. They encountered all kinds of theories that were based on isolated texts, but eventually they found formulae that would embrace all the texts. These formulae were not mere compromises but acute summaries that recognised the significance of all the relevant Biblical statements. In this way they arrived at the doctrine of the Trinity— that God is not a bare mathematical unity or a block of three—but three Centres of personal consciousness and activity. The Second Person of this Trinity became fully Man while remaining God; a single person with two spheres of activity. He fulfilled the purpose of His incarnation—His becoming Man—by dying for our sins and rising again to clear and empower us.

These formulae were stated in the standard Creeds, and these Creeds were accepted by all the Churches, Reformed and Unreformed, until fairly recently, as a true summary of what the Bible teaches. It is only in recent years that a change of attitude towards the Bible has resulted in criticisms of the Creeds. In this book we shall assume that the Christian revelation, as summarized in the Creeds, with its news of God's action in Christ, is so vital that it cannot be abandoned. It is not an option to be believed or discarded. For Christianity is not just a matter of doctrine. It has two other aspects, namely personal trust in the

Lord Jesus Christ as Saviour, and commitment to Him as Lord, borne out by a way of life, as we have already seen. There is considerable overlapping of moral behaviour between Christians and serious non-Christians, but the claim of Christian doctrine to be a body of revealed truth, and to show in Christ the bridge to God and, therefore, the way to goodness, is a claim unique among religions.

To return to the three categories with which we began this section:— any system that does violence to the Christian revelation is not an option, nor a hunting-ground for the sophisticated, but is something with which a Christian must not become involved. A Christian may marshal arguments against it and try to understand it, but he has to do this from outside and not from within.

All this means that, if experience shows that there are unusual happenings that can be labelled *occult*, a Christian not only looks to see whether they are beneficial or harmful, but tries to interpret them in the light of the total revelation given in Scripture. What, then, are these experiences that are called *occult*?

2. VISIBLE AND INVISIBLE

WE shall soon find that *occult* is a blanket word, and we shall need to break it down. Originally it simply means *hidden* or *invisible*, but it has obviously come to mean very much more than this. However, its literal use can help to lay a few foundations.

Men and women are part of a visible universe. Whatever views we hold about evolution or its extent, there is no doubt that human beings share many of the bodily functions of the animal world. So much so, that some scientists and psychologists suppose that man and his responses can be understood solely in animal terms.

The Bible uses the term *living creature* both of the non-human animal world (Genesis 1. 20, 24) and of the human (Genesis 2. 7). The identity of the Hebrew words is obscured by the AV with its translation 'man became a living soul', partially obscured by the RSV and Jerusalem Bible with 'man became a living being', but preserved by the NEB, which has 'living creature' in both places. The point of the other translations is to show that man is more than an animal; but it is best to keep the literal translation. Living creatures are of millions of different varieties. One has to gather from the rest of the Bible what sort of a living creature man is.

Meanwhile the Bible in Genesis 1 makes the point that there was first a creation of the mineral world, then of plants, and then of living creatures. Man shares in the mineral and plant world, but IS a living creature. It is impossible to live in this world unless one has physical substance of some kind. That is why, if Jesus Christ was to come to live in this world, He had to receive a physical body.

So much for the visible. The Bible, however, indicates that man stands between the visible and an invisible world. There is no doubt that, while man is an animal, there is a definite gap between every race of man and the rest of the animals. Man has a plus quality that separates him from them. He can be seen to differ from them genetically, and culturally, and in the mental realm. Only man has ideas, ideals or religions.

Suppose that some of this plus quality resembles the nature of another type of being. Starting at the top, the Bible shows that God made man in His own likeness. The Mormons may regard this as physical likeness, but the Bible does not say so. In this context the words of Genesis 1. 26-29 indicate capacity for ordering the world, and ruling as God's representative. To do this, man must have personality, and self-consciousness, and be capable of an over-riding and deliberate diversion of his mere animal instincts. Moreover, as the Genesis story unfolds, it shows that God and man can talk together. Man has animal life but he also has spiritual capacity.

It is difficult to use the terms 'soul' and 'spirit' consistently, since the Bible varies in its use of them. For example, the word translated *creature* in *living creature* is the Hebrew NEPHESH, which can also be translated *soul*. (There is a corresponding Greek

25

word PSYCHE with the same ambiguity.) For the moment I am keeping to its meaning of 'animal life'.

Similarly the Hebrew word RUACH is variously translated 'spirit', 'wind', 'breath'. For example, all three translations are essential in Ezekiel 37. 9, 14, as marginal notes will point out. Breath and wind are invisible energies, breath being the sustainer of life. The invisible centre of what we call *higher life* is also called *spirit* and the term is applied both to the human spirit and, supremely, to the bodiless Holy Spirit of God. This emerges clearly in Christ's conversation with Nicodemus, where we find the corresponding Greek word PNEUMA: 'That which is born of the Spirit is spirit' (John 3. 6). There is a deliberate play on words in verse 8, which can be kept in an English translation only by a marginal note to say that the word for 'wind' ('The wind blows where it wills') is the same as that translated 'spirit'.

If there are creatures that are purely animal, is it not possible that there are other creatures that are purely spirit? If man shares the one type of life, since he lives in the material world, does he share something of the other type also? The difficulty is that, if these other beings exist, they are invisible and undetectable by material instruments, just as God is, and just as the spirit of man is. Then how can we learn about them? Once again we must turn to the Bible as the source book of revelation about the invisible world *so far as it concerns us*. There are likely to be plenty of points we might wish to know, but we could no more understand them than the dragonfly larva, which lives entirely in the water, could understand the life of the air in which it will one day live.*

The Bible clearly confronts us with the sphere of the occult (hidden, invisible), for it emphatically states that God created a realm of spirits without physical bodies. This is not a very fashionable belief today, partly because we do not like to believe in anything that cannot be demonstrated by the physical sciences, partly because the existence of such beings does not necessarily help to explain natural phenomena, and partly perhaps because we have an underlying pride and feel that 'man is the greatest'.

However, the Bible says that such beings actually exist and that they come into a category between God and man. They are referred to as *sons of God* in Job 1. 6; 2. 1; 38. 7, probably in the sense that all are direct creations of God, and do not reproduce their kind as animals do (Matt. 22. 30). They are also called *angels*, which refers only to their duties: the Hebrew and Greek words both mean *messengers*. Some unseen beings are referred to as *spirits*, some as *evil spirits*. Evil spirits are also spoken of as *demons*, which is a transliteration of the Greek plural word DAIMONIA. Although the AV always translates this word as *devils*, the Greek actually uses the word for

*This analogy is lifted from Mrs. Gatty's *Parables from Nature*, one of the finest analogy books ever written. First published in 1855, it has been in print ever since.

devil (DIABOLOS) only in the singular to refer to the supreme spiritual rebel, Satan.

The Bible also speaks of grades of spirit beings. In visions of God in glory cherubim and seraphim stand by His throne (Isa. 6. 2; Ezek. 10), and angels (Rev. 4 and 5), and we hear also of Michael the Archangel (Jude 9). There is mention, too, of *principalities and powers;* in Titus 3. 1 the term is used of earthly rulers ('rulers and authorities' RSV), but elsewhere they are spiritual rulers, both good (Col. 1. 16) and rebellious (Eph. 6. 12; Col. 2. 15).

Angels are not departed spirits, as spiritualists hold. They existed before man was made (Job 38. 4-7). The saved in heaven do not become angels, but are 'like angels' in respect of not bearing children (Matt. 22. 30). God uses angels as His messengers, as He uses human beings. They serve those who are being saved (Heb. 1. 14; Acts 12. 7). They represent children in heaven (Matt. 18. 10). They form the heavenly court (Rev. 5. 11). In their duties they are simply the faithful agents of God, responsible to Him alone, and may not be worshipped or approached in their own right (Col. 2. 18-23; Rev. 22. 8, 9). In heaven they are wholly centred in God (Rev. 5. 11).

Some occultists profess to make use of them, and they also profess to contact other beings in between God and man. Thus they speak of Devas, who uphold various aspects of nature, elves, fairies, and undines (water spirits). If any such spirits exist, they come under the heading of 'the elemental spirits of the universe' (Col. 2. 20; Gal. 4. 3, 9, RSV and NEB). Christians are warned not to cultivate an interest in them, but rather exhorted to press on in union with the Head of the universe (Eph. 1. 20-23). Why dabble with inferior spirit powers when we can go to the Fountain Head? (Eph. 3. 17-21; Col. 2. 9, 10, 19).

3. GOOD AND BAD SPIRITS

IF there are both good and bad spirits, this is of considerable importance for our subject, since the occult apparently involves contact with the spirit world, and we need to know what kind of spirits are encountered. Indeed Christians are told to test spirit manifestations (1 Cor. 12. 3; 1 John 4. 1-3), and are warned against deception by spirits posing as good when in reality they are bad (1 Tim. 4. 1; 2 Cor. 11. 3, 4, 14, 15; Rev. 12. 9). If occult manifestations come from the spirit world, they must clearly be tested to know whether they are from a good or bad source. And since there are no physical instruments for making such tests, we are dependent on what the Bible says, and on what our God-given common sense deduces from the Bible. We want to know all that can be known with reasonable certainty, and we do not want to be deceived.

What then does the Bible say about good and bad spirits? But first we must go back to our earlier definitions of *good* and *bad*. The essence of *good* and *bad* in the Bible is harmony or lack of harmony with God. If we do not understand this, we run into difficulties over how a good God could create bad beings. There will always be a mystery about evil, but essentially evil is saying No to God.

Now, an animal cannot say this No. It normally lives within the circle of its instincts, or, as some may prefer to say, is governed by drives that are instigated by its tissue needs. An animal is close to being a mobile computer. So, indeed, is man, physically speaking, but for all practical purposes we do not regard him quite so clinically, though some have tried to do so. We prefer to treat ourselves and others as having an ability to turn things over in our minds, to consider abstract ideas and to exercise some power of choice that is over and above the drive of our tissue needs or the effects of inheritance and environment, powerful though these things are. We have, to all intents and purposes, the characteristics of free response.

God created, or brought into being, the static mineral world, the growing plant world, and the mobile animal world, each with its own limits. These limits did not include free response at a God-fellowship level. So God created human beings who could say Yes and No consciously and deliberately. An animal enjoys harmony through obeying its drives. Man has harmony by saying Yes to God; through controlling his drives by putting them under the direction of God. He is capable of being God-centred.

The story of the Fall in Genesis 3 is the story of a being, who once enjoyed harmony and intelligent friendship with God, but who opted out so that he could decide right and wrong for himself; in other words, he became self-centred instead of God-centred. If God had overridden man's free will and kept him as a puppet on a string, He could have prevented this; but that would have reduced man to the animal level, and God wanted one who would love Him deliberately and willingly. Thus man's first sin was in a sense negative—saying No. However, from the moment he shifted his control centre from God to himself, man's whole being began to function in a positively bad way. He was like a machine which falls out of alignment at the centre, but which is still connected to its active source of power. The negative lack of alignment then becomes positive damage. So God did not create evil, but He created free beings, who were genuinely free to say Yes or No to Him, but who, in saying No, disorganized themselves in a way that made them actively bad.

This is what the Bible says about man, and it makes sense in the light of experience. The Garden of Eden story describes how a wrong choice was made by the first full man and woman. It shows that *good* is saying Yes to God, and therefore being God-centred, and that *bad* is saying No, and taking control into our own hands. If some humanists think it is degrading to human nature to be dependent on God, they misunderstand the true position. The whole point is that God does not want us to be His puppets, but His friends. In spite of our limited outlook, we may know the all-knowing One who wants to go with us into the upheavals of the world.

So much for the human side. The Bible goes behind this, and shows that the bad was already there when man was created. The serpent was a cover for a spirit being who was already evil (Rev. 12. 9). We can apply to his fall the same principle which we saw in the fall of man, and say that this spirit being, whom we call Satan, was not created evil, nor is he an eternal god of evil, but he, like man, has said No to God; in his case, too, a negative response to God turned into a positive evil.

We shall work this out in the next chapter, but in the meantime we have reached a point where we can say that goodness and badness exist in the spirit world. Among human beings there is now a twist in all who are born: we refer to it as *original sin*. Since these other spirit beings do not intermarry and bear children (Matt. 22. 30), each is separately responsible for saying Yes or No to God and do not inherit this twist. They are free beings, and as such can appreciate the glory of God's creation (Job 38. 7; Isa. 6. 3) and fulfil their place in it (Heb. 1. 7). Yet evidently some have said No, and there is no evidence that any of these have turned back to God.

4. SATAN AND HIS WORKS

So far, then, we have seen that human beings are members of a visible and invisible creation. God has shown us in Scripture that there are non-physical, and normally invisible, beings, some good and some bad, which are, like ourselves, part of the same creation, and which are, like us, personal. When we speak of them as personal, let us be sure that we are not using mere imagery. We realize that some spiritual truths have to be conveyed to us under suitable imagery, since our physical experience makes it impossible for us to comprehend everything directly; 'Now we see in a mirror dimly', says Paul (1 Cor. 13. 12). But imagery must be such as to put our thoughts on to right lines. It is intended to be helpful, not misleading. If it is important for us to be aware of what goes on behind the scenes, we can be sure that God will have shown us what we need to know. So when Jesus Christ, with His actual experience of the invisible world, always speaks of Satan as personal, and when He rebukes demons as persons, we cannot suppose that He is teaching that these names simply represent an impersonal force of evil. Jesus Christ, and the Bible as a whole, speak of one personal devil, given the name Satan (the adversary), always in the singular, and of many demons.

Now, is Satan in any sense the evil counterpart of the God of absolute goodness? He is sometimes popularly imagined as such, but the Biblical picture differs from the popular view. Satan is not an eternally existing dark power, corresponding to the eternal light power, the true God. He is a created being, who appears as the chief rebel against God. God declares emphatically that He Himself is the sole Absolute. 'I am the first and I am the last; besides me there is no God' (Isa. 44. 6). Thus, Satan is not an absolute god of evil, even though he may assume the place of a god.

The Bible never denies that other beings and things may take the place of God in our devotion, and the Second Commandment tells us, 'You shall have no other gods before (or besides) Me' (Exod. 20. 3). When the Bible speaks in this way of 'other gods', it is admitting their reality in the sense that anything which becomes the object of our worship is, to us, a god, but it denies that this gives them equality of right with God to be proper objects of worship. There is also no idea that the Bible is inconsistent as to whether there is one God or many, different views being presented by different writers at different times. It is noteworthy that Jesus Christ Himself spoke of attempts to divide our allegiance between God and Mammon; He meant by this to warn us that we may be theological monotheists but practical polytheists (Matt. 6. 24).

We have seen, then, that Satan is personal, and that he is not absolute, and that he is evil. Since the good God would not have created a bad being, Satan must have fallen, just as the human race fell. Although there is no clear description of his original fall from God-centredness in the Bible, we find allusions to it in Isaiah 14. 12-20, and Ezekiel 28. 11-19, where two proud kings are described in terms of their master, who tried to usurp God's throne. (In Ezek. 28. 14, 16, follow AV, RV or NEB margin.) Satan, then, was not created evil, but is a fallen rebel, and it is his nature to desire that good should always fall. So he tempted men to fall from God-centredness too, and when they did so they came over, whether they realized it or not, on to his side. He is not, however, responsible for every sin of man, and, if he were to be blotted out at this moment, with all his evil associates in the spirit world, human beings would still continue to sin, because they also are rebels in their own right and have a twist in their make-up. Christians rightly speak of the three sources of temptation—not one—as 'The world, the flesh, and the devil'.

According to Scripture the primary aim of Satan is to organize a world system from which God is excluded. There is no reason to think he was lying when he told Jesus that all the authority and glory of the world system was his to give to anyone he wished (Luke 4. 6). But Jesus refused the gift, which would have meant power without salvation, and chose to go forward to the death on the cross that would cast out 'the ruler of this world' (John 12. 31, 32), who, in spite of all his efforts, could not fasten anything on the Saviour (John 14. 30). At the cross Jesus disarmed Satan and his associates by taking on Himself the sins which gave them a hold

on the human race (Col. 2. 14, 15). Yet Satan still
has power to blind human beings to the victory that
can free them. The most trenchant verses are
2 Cor. 4. 4, 'The god of this world has blinded the
minds of the unbelievers, to keep them from seeing
the light of the gospel of the glory of Christ, who is
the likeness of God'; and 1 John 5. 19, 'We know
that we are of God, and the whole world is in the
power of the evil one'.

Satan has assumed the position of god-substitute
for this world. The *world* in Scripture really means
materialism: the system of living that is organized
without God, and that acts on the assumption that
all reality is bounded by the horizons of birth and
death. We therefore live so as to get the maximum
out of this life, and lay up treasure on earth. Thus
the *world* is not the same as the *earth*, which in all
its fulness is the Lord's (Psalm 24. 1). The Bible does
not suggest that people are consciously aware of
Satan as their god. What Satan is concerned about
is that they should not turn to the only true God
by way of the Cross. Thus he throws a veil of darkness over men's minds (2 Cor. 4. 4) and 'deceives
the whole world' (Rev. 12. 9), often making the evil
course appear good (2 Cor. 11. 14; Gen. 3. 5).

If we can get the picture of Satan as the arch-
rebel who uses every possible weapon against God,
we shall find it easier to see his hand in the realm of
the occult. So long as we think of him as attacking
us only through our flesh, we shall miss much of the
subtlety of his working. Satan uses the world and the

37

flesh when it suits him, but he employs plenty of other tactics too.

More and more, we come to see Satan in the Bible as the twisted arch-humanist. Human humanists are often admirable people. They want to make this world a fit place for human beings to live in, and they want human beings to have freedom to develop as individuals and as members of society. But, sadly enough, their one condition is that they must do this without God. Thus they stop us from becoming truly human since they ban all that Jesus Christ has told us about God.

Satan takes these ideals and twists them. He tries to make man confuse freedom with self-centredness. He wants men to live in this world only on his terms: and his terms at this point coincide with the basic doctrines of humanism—that man should live without God, should be man-centred. But human nature is fallen and man-centredness soon becomes in the individual self-centredness and self-seeking. This can take many forms, some of them unexpected: it can range from the highest thinking of philosophy through aestheticism and on through the acquisition of material wealth and possessions to every kind of gross indulgence.

In Scripture, we mostly see Satan acting against the people of God who know God's distinctive message. He tries to crush Job. He fights to keep Jesus Christ from going to the Cross, first by rousing Herod to try and kill Him as a baby, then by tempting Him in the wilderness to take short cuts to get a following, and even to go shares with Him in running the world. Later he uses the emotional appeal of Peter to try to turn His mind from the Cross (Matt. 16. 21-23). When the Cross looms near, he tries to turn all the disciples away so that there will be no one to preach the Gospel (Luke 22. 31, N.B. the plural 'you').

He does not mind the elevated wisdom of the Greeks, since this rejects the Cross and the Resurrection (1 Cor. 1. 18-25; Acts 17. 32). Satan fears the Cross. This is not surprising, since on the Cross, as we have seen, Christ broke his power. The victory of the Cross has a twofold aspect. Jesus Christ, by bearing the sins of mankind, made it possible for them to escape from the evil, non-God, kingdom of Satan (e.g. Col. 1. 13-20). Also by doing so Christ took the headship of the human race, who had failed miserably as rulers and directors of the world over which God had appointed them (Gen. 1. 26-28). Jesus Christ was the first Man to live as the perfect Servant of His Father, and, although He died voluntarily as if He had been a sinner, His Resurrection turned His death into the supreme triumph. (One of the finest summaries of this is Philippians 2. 5-11.) Thus He took the right of rule from Satan, the usurper. Christ's people go out in the power of this victory, and the Holy Spirit within them is their living link with Him. Yet God has not exterminated Satan, and he still continues the struggle, maybe hoping that he may yet find a way to outwit God.

He might try to get his way by killing many of the Church, and frightening the rest into denying their faith. Thus the New Testament names him as the stirrer-up of persecutions. He is like the lion roaring after its prey (1 Peter 5. 8-10). He or his representatives try to force idolatrous submission under threat of death (Rev. 13. 11-18). Yet by the providence of God he has never stamped out any single generation of Christians. In fact his efforts have given rise to the epigram that the blood of the martyrs is the seed of the Church.

We must, however, listen to the warnings of Christ and the New Testament writers that Satan has another line of attack, namely persuading the Church to shift from the basic revealed beliefs. Jesus Christ warned of false messiahs and false prophets who would be a menace to the faith of the Church (Matt. 24. 23, 24). Although Satan is not mentioned here by name, it is clear from the Epistles that Satan is in fact the propagator of these attractive, anti-Christian ideas. He has his ministers who pose as being on the side of righteousness (2 Cor. 11. 13-15). He can make them appear to be inspired prophets (1 John 4. 1-6). He lays traps for Christians, and the property of a trap is that it appears to be normal and good until it is sprung (1 Tim. 3. 7 and 2 Tim. 2. 26). His attacks are represented as crafty wiles, and wiles are by nature deceptive (Eph. 6. 11. The word occurs again in 4. 14). The Book of Revelation is intended to throw light on Satan's methods, since he is the deceiver of the whole world (12. 9), and the Book repeatedly warns against giving way before persecution or embracing false doctrines (e.g. in the Letters to the Churches in chapters 2 and 3).

All this is highly relevant to our subject. So-called Satanism is certainly grossly immoral, and Christians are hardly likely to plunge into it. But if we accept the fact that Satan is primarily concerned to divert us into alternatives to the Gospel, then we must be prepared for him to offer these alternatives in the form of plausible psychic and spiritual experiences. For those who deify the intelligence of man, he has other alternatives again, although he may use temptations at the one level to bolster up those at the other.

Thus the Scriptures expose the concerted schemes against God which in the sphere of spirits lurk behind the scenes of world history. For His own reasons God allows fallen spirits to continue in existence just as He allows fallen man. But wherever God's work of grace and redemption appears, these schemers try to undo it. Since they have had long experience, and their awareness of situations is greater than man's, they are stronger than man. They can be thrown back only when a Christian clothes himself in the spiritual and moral armour of God (Eph. 6. 10-18) and claims the Name and victory of Jesus Christ (Acts 16. 18; Eph. 1. 19-23), realizing that already he shares with Christ in His reign (Eph. 2. 6).

5. MAN AS BODY AND MIND

So invisible (occult) beings exist, and a whole host of them are active for evil in the universe of which we also are part. Since they regard God as their enemy, and since He is particularly concerned to bring human beings into the maturity of union with Himself, they will interfere with His work, directly and indirectly, whenever they can, and we should expect them both to attack and to use mankind when it suits them.

Now, the fact remains that we are different in kind from them, just as we differ from fleas and lions. There is some common ground between ourselves, fleas and lions, since all have physical and visible bodies. How much common ground can there be between ourselves as bodies and those who are spirits without bodies? We shall need two chapters, first to sort out body and mind, and then to go deeper into non-material realms that bear some resemblance to spirit existence.

During the past hundred years the rapid development of suitable techniques and instruments has given us a completely new vision of the human body and brain. One dare not even mention some of these amazing discoveries for fear of giving this book an old-fashioned look in a few years' time. But some think it possible to write a book on human personality and behaviour without going beyond the physical. More and more man is being depicted as the supreme computer, which is to be kept in working order by a proper balance of pills and medicines and triggered controls. Christians must not challenge this view of man as being totally wrong. It is certainly right as a description of a vital aspect of human life, but it is not the whole truth.

In chapter 2 we noted that man has a link both with the world of spirit life and with the world of animal life. As regards physical life, he is animal and mineral, and is wholly dependent on the vegetable world for his continuity of life, as every boy and girl has had demonstrated at school. There are certain fundamental conditions of an existence of this kind. Such an existence has to be largely controlled automatically by the kind of negative feedback system that forms the basis of modern computers. Thus, for instance, a severe cut will automatically set a whole train of events in motion, each in turn triggering off others, so that the body is affected to the minimum possible degree and the bleeding stops. Any departure from the 'normal' occasions repairs, adjustments, and compensations in the body. Similar effects can be studied in the animal world in general, and can be incorporated into machines.

If we say that a person is a body, we are not denying anything in the Bible. We should be if we added the word *only*, but we shall not do that. Certainly the Bible treats man as a body, and in the New Testament the word *body* occurs 145 times. *Spirit* occurs some 40 times of the human spirit, and sometimes it is debatable whether it refers to the Holy Spirit indwelling the Christian. *Soul* is used some 50 times of an inner and persisting something in addition to the body; sometimes also it is used in the sense of *an individual*, or as *animal life*.

Whatever the exact figures, the fact is clear that the body is to be treated neither as an enemy nor as the whole man, but is to be the temple of the Holy Spirit, in which we are to bring glory to God (1 Cor. 6. 20). Christians have sometimes failed to see this. Our animal body is an essential part of us, and we cannot normally fly in the face of those animal body laws that are summed up by such words as food, rest, exercise.

We recognize also that we have three primary drives that are found in the rest of the animal world, and are needed to maintain each kind of animal in existence. These are sex, for the perpetuation of the species; self-preservation for the continued existence of the individual for as long as necessary; and group drive, for the preservation of society. This last belongs to all animals who need to live as a society. All these drives can be interpreted as physical.

And yet, when we have said all this, we know that we are not simply animals. There is a delightful summary by the psychologist David Katz in *Animals and Men* (Pelican). 'It is in his childhood that man is most subject to the influence of instincts. In later life behaviour is so much more controlled by external forces that its instinctive basis can hardly be distinguished any longer. Unlike the animals, he does not pass his life within the security of his instincts. He has the power to shape it for himself' (p. 173).

It is true that some levels of society, modern society included, challenge this by their behaviour. 'Permissive society' involves a descent into the purely animal, so that physical drives break out into action as soon as they make themselves felt. Indiscriminate sex divorced from family ties; drugs and drink that inflate self before becoming destructive of the self; grouping in small herds at the expense of society as a whole—all these things appear to one of the older generation trying to be understanding, to be the logical result of treating a human being as no more than a machine with built-in immediate responses. We become more animal, and less natural, if by *natural* we mean *truly human*.

There are still, however, many people, Christians and non-Christians, who take man a step further. We cross the threshold at the point where physical stimuli are turned into something wholly different. This is the mystery of consciousness, which no one has yet solved. Briefly, every physical stimulus (sight, hearing, touch, etc.) sets up the equivalent of an electrical current that travels along the appropriate nerves to the brain. Every current appears to be essentially the same, but, according to the place in the brain where it ends, so it is transferred into colour, sound, feeling, etc. We do not perceive the world as it is to the physical sciences—roughly a series of waves—but as a world of people and things.

We go a step further, and enter the sphere of ideas, pictorial and non-pictorial. We can close our eyes and shut out the avenue of the senses, and build

45

up pictures directly in our mind. We can discuss abstract ideas such as goodness, truth, beauty, and religion.

It is not easy to say at what point we pass from the purely animal to the fully human. Personally I avoid picturing man as a pile of blocks: 'this block represents the body: on top of that is the mind: on top again is the spirit'. This splits man in a non-Biblical way, and forces us into unnecessary arguments with science and psychology. If we diagrammatically draw a human being as a spiral, we are on surer ground. If the body is at the bottom of the spiral, i.e. grounded on the earth, somewhere along the coil we merge into that conscious awareness of the world and of ourselves that we call Mind. We are now in a sphere of living that is beyond the purely animal world, even though it is securely linked to the animal. We are in the realm of personal choice, remembering again that many of our responses are physical habits.

Although some psychologists and philosophers hold in theory that all human behaviour and thinking can be explained as the physical and built-in responses of something like an intricate animal computer, they write their books as though their readers can be intelligently persuaded to accept what they present as the truth. Curiously enough, they often criticize Christians for producing pressure conversions by triggering off responses at evangelistic campaigns. If this were how conversions happen, Christians would merely be acting on what these behaviourist psychologists have taught them to do, i.e. treat your hearers like machines! As Dr. Joad used to point out, truth on this basis becomes a meaningless term, since your built-in responses force you to make certain pronouncements, while mine force me to make a different set, and there is no significance in weighing one against the other and saying that one is true and the other false! If, however, the words *true* and *false* are given secondary meanings of *expedient* and *inexpedient*, you may cleverly bend my mind by playing on my habit responses, or by offering rewards and punishments, or by drugs, or by interference with my brain, and in this way make me see 'truth' and come out of my 'error'. This is one of the most horrible clouds that hangs over the human race at present. We already succumb to it in the field of advertising. Yet even the slick advertisement has to admit some capacity to choose, and has to *persuade* us that the advertised product is *better* than another, for some end that we have been taught to regard as desirable.

At present, then, the human race recognizes that it can be degraded to animal-reaction level, and it resists this with all its power of apparently free choice. We as Christians believe that in this the common sense of the common man is fundamentally correct. The alternative sequel belongs to horror science fiction.

Just as we have said that man IS body, so let us say that man IS mind. This means that he has self-awareness, and can draw together his fragmentary day-by-day world experiences in a meaningful way. In the light of these he can weigh up his end and aim, and can realize that some of his physical habit responses need to be checked or modified if he is to aim constructively at a goal. He also finds himself in a world of values, to which he applies words like *good, true, beautiful, just*. Here *right* and *wrong* take on a different meaning from *beneficial* or *harmful*. He may differ from some of his fellows on what acts are right or wrong, but he is prepared to discuss this as something to be settled intelligently and not simply by feeling. What he is clear about is that it is never right to do wrong or wrong to do right!

6. FROM MIND TO SPIRIT

WE have looked at those capacities that man has in common with the animal world and those in which he differs from other animals. Can we now also look at man in relation to spirit beings?

In the previous chapter we regarded the mind as what a person is as regards his rational awareness and evaluative thinking. We have thus avoided having to treat Mind as an entity, a thing in itself. Yet we know that we are not simply rational assessors of life. Our consciousness is commonly compared to the visible tip of an iceberg, which is only a small part of the total block.

Let us start with your present awareness. At this moment you are aware of two or three things in addition to this book that you are reading. Below the surface there are a great many things that can be brought out when we need them. They are stored memories. Below these are the other experiences of our life that are certainly stored, but they cannot be recalled when we want them. Also below the conscious level we are aware of seething forces that often impel or retard us. If ever we need to consult a depth psychiatrist, he will treat us on the assumption that some unknown tensions are affecting our conscious actions, and the probability is that he will unearth these by bringing some buried memory or fear into the light of day.

He will probably work upon the basic assumption that infancy attitudes, particularly in relation to our parents, have produced feelings, including ideas of guilt, that have been repressed into forgetfulness, but still make themselves felt with their childhood energies. They may come out under stress, or they may produce a life style which makes us view all situations as if, for example, we are bound to be dependent on some parent figure.

Freud emphasized guilt repression, broadly linked to the sex instinct in its infancy. Adler saw the life style formed by the urge for superiority or the fear of inferiority. Jung saw not only the repressions but also the dynamic movement for health and wholeness below the conscious level. Others, such as Frankl, speak of the inner urge to make sense of life's experiences. If we are wise we shall draw upon all these ideas.

If we call this level of the mind the *Unconscious*, we are asserting that its contents are not normally accessible to our consciousness. If we again speak in personal terms we may say that *I am* at an unconscious level, as well as *I am* body and conscious mind. Once again this may keep us from thinking of our Unconscious as a separate cellar.

We can investigate this sphere only with great difficulty. But we must not overlook this part of ourselves, because it may influence our life in unusual ways; we have already noted the effect of repressions. We can regard it also as the promoter of some dreams. The dynamic of genius and aesthetic inspiration, too, must be linked to unconscious receptivity in the first instance. Beside this, there is for the Christian the point that the indwelling of the Holy Spirit belongs to this level of experience as well as affecting the other levels.

This last point is important. The New Testament regards the Holy Spirit as coming to 'live' within the Christian when he or she is linked to Christ in the New Birth (e.g. 1 Cor. 6. 19, 20). Christ spoke to Nicodemus about the Holy Spirit bringing new life to the spirit of man (John 3. 6), and He compared the Holy Spirit to a fountain rising within and flowing out (John 7. 37-39). The Epistles, notably Romans 8, speak repeatedly of the Holy Spirit coming to live within the Church and the individual Christian, although we must be clear that nowhere in the New Testament is the Holy Spirit said to be in all mankind.

We saw that, while we cannot directly perceive the contents of our Unconsciousness, we are aware of the dynamic forces that flow from it and affect our conduct and thinking. If the human spirit, which can receive the Holy Spirit, is one aspect of our Unconscious, then we can see how we do not directly perceive the Holy Spirit, but we become aware that He is there. We can thus add to our pronouncements, *I am* spirit, meaning that I can function in yet another direction. In saying this, we have kept the unity of our personality, our I, so that we see how one sphere of our being is bound to influence the others. There is no such thing as a new birth in the spirit that does not make both possible and necessary the transformation of the mind

(Rom. 12. 2) and body (1 Cor. 6. 19, 20), and there is no action of the body that does not affect the mind and spirit (Phil. 3. 18-21). This is because *I am* functionally body, mind, and spirit, and I cannot block off one 'section' and refuse to recognize it.

In the previous chapter we wrote of psychologists of a behaviourist type who believe that man can be understood and treated somewhat like a mobile computer. If they have little place for the concept of a free consciousness, they have even less place for the unconscious mind. Thus H. J. Eysenck has no time for the ideas of the analysts, and of the three books by him that I have on my shelves, the word *Unconscious* does not appear at all in the index of any at all. Similarly much of Christian experience, particularly the experience of conversion, has been taken out of the realm of the spiritual, and naturalized, by William Sargant in *Battle for the Mind*.

We bear the cautions of such thinkers in mind, but believe we can go further than they do. Certainly a Christian *is* body, and cannot detach himself from the mechanisms of body and brain. This applies equally to his spiritual experiences, but that is not to deny that spiritual experiences exist in their own right: it is just that they do not exist in a vacuum. Neither does it mean that the spiritual does not build on the physical. We recognize that the mechanisms that operate in conversion to Communism or to some other ideal in adolescence must also be active in Christian conversion. The unifying pull of an ideal, good or bad, may change conduct.

In so far as Christ is an Ideal, as Philippians 3. 10 indicates that He is, ideal-mechanisms come into play. The difference is that Christ first offers forgiveness and a cleaning-away of sin, and then gives us a real life-link, to the deepest level, with God, through the indwelling of His Holy Spirit. Notice the importance of the truth of the Trinity here, especially as it emerges through the careful use of pronouns in John 14. 16-23.

There is a further hypothesis, which has much to commend it. It is connected especially with the psychologist, Jung, who postulates a Collective Unconscious in which the Individual Unconscious shares. Let us try to put it personally again. *I am* at an unconscious level, and *I am* also humanity. This being human is more than belonging to a club: it is sharing in the present existence and the past experiences of the whole human race, and we must regard this sharing as being in the sphere of the Unconscious. It explains the universality of certain symbols, which emerge in dreams, in the mind through psycho-analysis, and in folk stories, irrespective of nation or of time. It explains the way in which ideas can catch on from one person to another, even across the nationality-barrier. And it puts the Christian on the track of how Jesus Christ could in reality bear the past, present, and future sins of mankind. For, when He became incarnate, He became incorporated into the whole human race, whose unity is not simply physical but deep in a corporate Unconscious. We are not normally aware of this unity, or link, but, like our personal Unconscious, it may influence us. Jesus Christ was able to become incorporated in this 'soul' of humanity without becoming personally contaminated by it, although, when He bore the sins of the world, He must in some mysterious way have gathered up all its existence, bad and good, in Himself. We could almost say that the life of the world died on the Cross in the death of Christ, who is its Creator and Upholder (Col. 1. 17-20; Heb. 1. 2, 3). This was symbolized by the blacking out of the sun, the light of the world (Matt. 27. 45).

This may start you thinking if you have not seen it in this way before; but, if it is not something that makes sense to you, then leave it for the time being. The vital thing is the *fact* that Christ died for our sins, and not the *theory* of all that was involved in His death.

7. PSYCHIC OR OCCULT?

WE have pictured a human being as a coiled spiral, with one aspect of his existence merging into another without any blocked-off division. We worked from the physical, through the mental, to the spiritual, noting several overlaps on the way. Particularly we noted that the label *unconscious* covers several aspects of a man, and that these aspects may need differing treatment. Their common factor is that they are difficult to perceive directly, although we postulate their existence because of certain effects that emerge in our conscious lives.

It might make the spiral picture too complicated if we joined up the ends and made a ring coil, and yet this would reinforce what we have been trying to say. The picture as we left it in the previous chapter might still produce the common conception that the spirit is at the other end of the line from the body, whereas in fact every part of the spiral has a two-way link with any other part. Anything that happens anywhere in the circle flows in every direction.

So long as we recognize this, we can analyze individual aspects, just as a biologist can analyze a section of the human body, provided he realizes that the section is a vital part of the whole. The Bible thinks of the whole, while recognizing the parts. Thus Paul writes in 1 Thessalonians 5. 23: 'May the God of peace Himself sanctify you wholly; and may your spirit and soul and body be kept sound and blameless at the coming of our Lord Jesus Christ'.

The word *occult* means *hidden*, but not everything that is hidden is necessarily occult. The word is not used of every aspect of the hidden Unconscious. It is applied to certain strange phenomena that emerge spontaneously, or are produced deliberately, from some hidden source. They are strange because they are not subject to the laws of the physical and mental realms by which we consciously live and which we apply to the understanding of life. *Occult* has a more sinister sound than *psychic*, which in more scientific writing nowadays is often shortened to *psi*, the Greek letter Ψ.

It is often easier to get the feel of word usage than it is to define it closely, but probably one may say that *psychic* speaks of apparent non-physical, yet human, powers that emerge under certain conditions. These would be primarily telepathy, clairvoyance, and precognition (becoming aware of the future). We might include some supernormal healing powers, faculties of water or metal divining, and the ability to see auras of colour or light around the human body. Later we must consider whether it is right to develop these faculties.

The word *occult*, on the other hand, suggests contact with spirit powers, consequent magic and witchcraft. It is impossible to draw a hard line between the two, because the occult may include the psychic. If there is contact with spirits, these spirits may use the latent powers of man, and we shall sometimes be faced not only with human beings using their latent human powers, but also with spirits making use of these powers through those who possess them: that is, we shall be faced with *both/and*, as well as *either/or*.

We can illustrate with the phenomenon of the *do-it-yourself* occultism of the ouija board or the inverted tumbler. There has been an outbreak of this type of 'communication' in the last few years, especially in schools and colleges. The general principle is that a small group of people rest their fingers lightly on an inverted tumbler, or small board with legs or castors, which is on a smooth table. On the outside of the table there are letters of the alphabet and figures, and simple words like Yes and No. In due course the tumbler or small board spells out answers to questions. The tumbler itself does not give the answers, but the communications come in the name of some spirit who professes to be someone who has passed on.

An earlier form of communication that was popular in the middle of the last century was table tipping. Here a circle of people rested their hands on a table, often a very solid one, and asked questions of the spirits. They then called through the letters of the alphabet, and the table tilted when the appropriate one was reached. It was a slow process to spell out a sentence in this way. There is nothing new about the ouija board. The name was, I think, a trade name, and consists of the French *oui* and the German *ja,* both meaning *yes*. The first dictionary reference to the word appeared in 1904, but the writer is there alluding to it as something with which his readers would be acquainted.

When one has eliminated deliberate fraud by some member of the group, there is still the possibility of unconscious pushing. This could be eliminated by securely blindfolding everyone who is taking part, and then altering the order of the letters. Sir William Barrett in his book, *On the Threshold of the Unseen* (Kegan Paul, 1918), wrote of some experiments that he and some friends carried out in Dublin. Here answers were spelled out at high speed when the sitters had their eyes blindfolded and the alphabet letters were turned round. When the letters were jumbled, the movement of the indicating board was at first very slow, but it continued to spell out messages, and gradually speeded up.

We may stay with Barrett, since the messages he records are typical. Some could be substantiated: names and addresses of people who had recently died, and who were unknown to any of the group, were correctly given. There was a remarkable case on the day when the *Lusitania* sank. The group had heard the preliminary report but did not know that a personal friend of theirs, Sir Hugh Lane, was on board. A message was spelled out, 'Pray for the soul of Hugh Lane', and a description followed in the first person of his last minutes before he was drowned. A few minutes later they read his name in the evening paper's list of passengers. Subsequently the alleged Hugh Lane wrote about his will, but failed to explain an important codicil which was disputed!

The communicator who claimed to have introduced Hugh Lane to the ouija board gave his name as Peter Rooney. He told how he had led a life of crime and imprisonment in Boston, and had committed suicide ten days previously by throwing himself under a tram there. Barrett at once made enquiries from the police in Boston, Lincolnshire, and Boston, Massachusetts, but no such person as Peter Rooney was known, although several years ago a Peter Rooney had fallen from the elevated railway in Boston, Massachusetts, and was laid up for a month: he was still living in Boston.

To turn to a modern example: The papers recently got hold of the story of a seance arranged by some of the boys at a Blackpool school. An extract from a taped interview with one of the boys was published in the Inter-School Christian Fellowship periodical *Viewpoint* for Autumn 1970. The school is in an area which was the scene of several murders in the past, and the seance was held in a cellar in the school. The boys used an ouija board to contact the spirits, and received a communication which claimed to be from a woman murdered in 1854 by a man called Mercer. She claimed that an evil presence in the cellar was trying to impede her contact with the group. When she was asked to prove her presence, the temperature of the room began to fall. Although the board told them not to leave the cellar, some of the boys became frightened and the seance broke up.

One further illustration comes from a missionary

who on an evangelistic tour in England stayed at the home of a Christian lady who had formerly been a spiritualist. He was shown a broken ouija board on the bedroom shelf, and his hostess told him that she had once used it, but had become more and more suspicious of the origin of the messages that came through. Eventually she asked, 'I am perplexed: what shall I do?' The answer was spelled out, 'Trust and obey, for there's no other way to be happy in Jesus but to trust and obey'. The words are those of the chorus of a well-known evangelical hymn. However, she pressed further and asked, 'Who are you?' The answer came back, 'The Devil', upon which the leg of the board snapped and it collapsed. It seems strange that the lady kept the board, and this may be one reason why she told the missionary that she was still troubled by evil spirits, even in Church during the Communion service.

Here then are a few typical occurrences, a crazy mixed bag of obviously true, false, and doubtful communications. Is there any single explanation of them, or are we in the realm of multiple agencies? Are they psychic, or are they occult? Are they just the product of latent faculties in man or of the control of these faculties by unseen spirits?

8. PSYCHIC WITHOUT OCCULT

WE have three possible interpretations of the phenomena that we have taken as an illustration. They may be due to the emergence of latent powers in those who are taking part, or they may be produced by spirits. Or we may combine the two, and say that spirits are able to mobilize the latent powers in man, and direct them to their own ends.

The average person jumps straight to the second explanation, and certainly more Christians agree with them that spirits are responsible, but disagree over the identity of the spirits in question. Nevertheless I want to argue for the first and third.

Popular belief has always accepted the occurrence of occasional second sight. Until recently no one has seen how to devise the sort of repeatable experiments that a scientist needs if he is to investigate any occurrence. However, nowadays most people have heard of the work initiated by Dr. J. B. Rhine of Duke University in America. Dr. Rhine tested the ability of subjects to discover by telepathy the order of cards in a pack that someone else at a distance was turning up card by card. The cards had five special designs, and it was possible to find whether mathematically the results were above what would be expected by chance. Dr. Rhine obtained highly significant results with certain subjects after many runs through the pack.

In Britain the most useful book on this subject for the ordinary reader is the well-documented record, *The Mind Readers* (Faber and Faber 1959) by S. G. Soal and H. T. Bowden. The experimenters in this book tested two Welsh country boys of 14, who had the faculty of telepathic communication. They were tested in front of stage telepathists, who knew all the tricks. One of their greatest successes was on a cricket field, where they sat about eighty feet apart, and with a screen between them; they were first thoroughly searched for such things as concealed transmitters. On this occasion, on runs through shuffled packs of 25 cards of 5 different animal pictures, they obtained scores of 19, 20, 23, and 25 in successive runs; and this was not the only occasion on which they obtained high scores. Unfortunately the boys lost their gift in adolescence, and it has now been suggested that they used supersonic dog whistles in their mouths or clothing; but in view of the constant observation and searching they underwent, it is virtually impossible that such a whistle should not have been detected or heard by someone else.

If, then, telepathy, or thought reading, is a fact, it means that there can be a link-up of minds at a deep level, and that some of the contents of one mind can emerge into the consciousness of another. It can be used for practical purposes. Thus, we are told that telepathy is a regular occurrence among some of the Lapplanders who use it to make appointments to meet in the desolate wilds of their countryside.

So it is now impossible to read any serious

discussion of spiritualism without encountering the theory of telepathy. The reason why I use the term *spiritualism* in this book is not only for courtesy but because the alternative, *spiritism*, which some Christians prefer, suggests that all seance phenomena come directly from spirits. Certainly most mediums assume that they contact the spirits of those who have passed on, and that these spirits then give them messages to relay to someone in the room. But, if telepathy is a fact, why should not the medium be picking up the picture, voice, and message latent in the mind of the recipient?

An important figure in the field of psychical research is Mrs. Eileen Garrett, and she has been looking for an answer to this question for most of her life. In two of her books of autobiography, *My Life as a Search for the Meaning of Mediumship* (Rider, 1939), and *Many Voices* (Allen & Unwin, 1968), she believes that the alleged controlling spirits, with their distinctive voices and names, are facets of her own personality, and that the communications are built up in picture and voice form from the deep levels of her client's mind. In the second book she even expresses doubt about her own survival after death—which must be unique in a medium!

The telepathy theory is borne out by tests that have been tried from time to time. If an investigator goes to a seance with a fictitious relative or friend in mind, or if he meditates on some character in history or fiction, the medium may reproduce his thoughts in the form of a message from or description of the person in the client's mind. In one case a well-known medium at a public meeting picked up a name, Bessie White, who had been invented by one of her clients at a private seance twenty-one months previously. She took up where she had left off, although she had not seen the client between the two meetings, and is unlikely to have recognized her in the large audience.*

Investigators who visit various mediums find that, if one gets on the wrong tack, others will follow. A relative of mine was told some years ago by three different fortune tellers that she would die in a car crash at the age of thirty. I am glad to say that she is now past that age. The wrong intuition of the first psychic was picked up as fact by the others.

It is not easy to draw a line between telepathy and clairvoyance, and there is not much point in doing so. Telepathy is the awareness of what is in the mind of someone else, while clairvoyance is the direct perception of something that nobody is aware of. Both exclude normal perception through the senses. If I become aware of a picture that you are looking at a hundred miles away, that is assumed to be telepathy. If you place a shuffled pack of cards face downwards on the table, without you or anyone else knowing the order of the cards, and I then write down the order correctly, that is called clairvoyance.

Unfortunately the distinction is complicated by precognition, or awareness of the future. In extra-

*The case is recorded by K. M. Goldney in *Proceedings of the Society for Psychical Research*, Vol. XIV, 210-216.

sensory perception (ESP), such as telepathy and clairvoyance exhibit, the mind obviously transcends space, since it communicates at a distance without any physical means. But it has been found that ESP also transcends time. Experimentally this has been shown by the ability to get more than a chance average in calling the order of cards as they will be when they are subsequently shuffled. So my supposed clairvoyance may in fact be a telepathic reading of your mind as it will be when you check the order of the cards. Experimental precognition has confirmed popular belief that some people on occasions can see into the future.

There is an extension of telepathy known as psychometry. A few people have this capacity to take an object belonging to a person unknown to them, and then to become aware of the appearance of the owner or usual handler, and can see something of their past, present, and future. Experiments with such people were described fully by Dr. Eugene Osty in his book *Supernormal Faculties in Man*, translated from the French in 1923 (Methuen).

Having mentioned precognition, we reach a convenient point at which to take a brief look at techniques for discovering the future. Popular methods are by cards, tea leaves, palmistry, and astrology. The cards may be ordinary playing cards, but there is an increasing use of the Tarot pack of 78 cards, including 22 of highly symbolic pictures. The inquirer shuffles the pack with certain questions in mind, and the laying out of the cards answers these questions. It is thought that the *psi* faculty, which appears to have some reach outside of space and the progress of time, influences the arrangement of the pack, while additionally the reader's clairvoyant skill will interpret the signs, as with Osty's psychometry experiments. This may well be so.

Similarly the reader of the tea leaves undertakes what is not unlike a Rorschach inkblot test on the inquirer's behalf. This psychological test is a series of standard inkblots which the patient is asked to see as pictures. What he sees reflects his own personality. Similarly a clairvoyant reader of tea leaves may see them as pictures from the inquirer's mind, which may contain an awareness of the future.

Although palmistry and astrology have precise rules of working, the way readings are applied to individual clients varies from reader to reader. A sensitive clairvoyant is more likely to arrive at a correct delineation in palmistry, but, so far as the readings of day-to-day astrology are concerned, I find that they are of more use in showing after the event how the position of the planets 'influenced' certain happenings, rather than in predicting what will happen. In this they are comparable to some psychologists, who can cheerfully explain after the event exactly why so-and-so was converted at a particular meeting!

Is there anything wrong in trying to read the future? Well, if God has made us so that we naturally move through time step by step, can He mean us to use strange artificial methods, which admittedly are hit-or-miss, to find out what is to come to us?

I do, however, admit my belief that in some way we carry within us some of our future as well as our past, even though we cannot as yet formulate any agreed scientific or philosophical human time-map on which such a thing can be credibly demonstrated. And precognitive dreams and visions certainly do occur, even if these are no more than descriptively accurate dreams of a place which one has not yet visited (as happened to someone I know). God has disclosed certain future crises in the Bible, and from time to time He shows us, or grants us intuition of, some coming event in our own lives. This may simply come to us through some experience or situation and become meaningful when later we encounter the someone or the something else for which God was preparing us. The first experience has been a divine preparation for the second.

This, however, is different from our deliberately peering into the future, and there is a special danger for those who are serious practitioners of the Tarot. The devotee is called upon to pass through a mystical identification with each of the pleasant and unpleasant pictures on the cards. Even the dabbler suffers, and a student told me how he had to change his rooms because of the sense of evil that was released when his fellow students continually consulted the Tarot for guidance. Moreover, in constantly living by the Tarot, these students caused their proper capacities for decision-making to atrophy.

One other natural capacity ought to be mentioned before assessing the ouija board. This goes by the name of *cryptomnesia,* or latent memory. Many things that we have completely forgotten can be recalled under hypnotism. Moreover, items that we are not aware of having seen can be stored in our memories. Thus there has been considerable discussion on the morality of subliminal advertising, since tests have shown that a slogan flashed during a programme on the T.V. or cinema screen for too brief a period to register on the conscious mind, has penetrated sufficiently to create a response via the deeper part of the mind.

Could this factor have a bearing on the examples quoted in the previous chapter? The names and addresses of two people who had recently died may well have come from cryptomnesia, if a member of the group had noticed the announcement in the paper. A case in point took place in the last century, when Stainton Moses received a communication purporting to come from a certain Abraham Florentine, who had fought in the American war of 1812, and who had died at Brooklyn on August 5th 1874, aged 83 years, 1 month and 17 days. These details were correct, except that his actual age had been 83 years, 1 month and 27 days, as his widow testified. This may seem like an unimportant accidental slip in a single figure, but this same slip had already been made in Florentine's obituary notices in two American papers. It is therefore likely that Stainton Moses had in fact seen a copy of one of the papers although the obituary notice had not registered on his conscious mind.

There may be another explanation, too, for the mysterious Peter Rooney: he may have been a creation from the inspirational depths of someone's mind, who was forthwith adopted by the subconscious of the group as a real character. The boys who met in the school cellar were admittedly meeting in a place of bad repute, and they were likely to pick up something—not necessarily someone—from the past, a picture drawn from the imaginative depths of the boys' minds. One could go further, and on the lines of the experiments in psychometry say that some evil happenings had been imprinted on the surroundings, and were picked up by the released faculties of the boys.

This theory of imprinting is a perfectly good hypothesis to account for some hauntings. Generally a haunting centres in a person, or people, who had passed through some highly emotional experience, such as murder or torture, or who had been emotionally attached to a house. We need not suppose that they return personally in order to be murdered once again, but rather that some people, who can tune in to the right 'wave', perceive the person or event over again.

In his autobiography, *Behind the Brass Plate* (Sampson Low, 1928), Dr. A. T. Schofield relates how he went to a country house with a Christian lady who had second sight. While they were sitting in the hall, this lady suddenly jumped up and called to him to stop two men whom she saw fighting violently in the further corner of the hall. Dr. Schofield saw nothing, but, when the hostess appeared, she took it all quite calmly, and said that others had seen the same thing. The two men were a father and son who had lived some 200 years before.

Sometimes I am asked for Scriptural evidence for this theory of imprinting as an explanation of haunting. It is impossible to produce any, since Scripture never mentions haunting. All that we can do, therefore, when we encounter what seems to be a haunting, whether harmless or violent (as with poltergeists), is to produce a hypothesis that makes sense and that does not run counter to Scripture in other respects. So, if we say that imprinting accounts for some hauntings, we have a sensible theory. Probably one sees the event as one would have seen it from the same approximate position when it happened, but it is possible that such temporary second sight builds on the 'picture', and actually produces in us the emotions of the participants, as happens with psychometry.

Occasionally imprinting is picked up during the lifetime of the original participants. A story which was told me by someone whose opinion I trust is of a lady gifted with second sight, who went to stay with a family she had not previously met. As she came downstairs to dinner, the clock struck seven, and she saw a bearded man come in at the front door, while from one of the downstairs rooms a group of children ran out and flung themselves into his arms. Next moment all had vanished. It turned out that what she had seen was the grandfather, now dead, as he used to come home when his children were young, and the scene which commonly took place every evening at seven. The significance of the story is that, although grandfather was dead, all or most of the children were still alive as grown men and women.

To return to the boys, there may well have been a man named Mercer who murdered a woman in the cellar, but we need not suppose that she had returned from the dead to speak through the ouija board.

The Hugh Lane communicator is slightly different. Evidence is undeniable that round about the time of death, as well as during illness or at some crisis, a person has appeared or spoken to some relative or friend at a distance. One accepts the fact, but is puzzled by the mechanism involved. It is all very well to say that my friend actually appeared to me at the moment of his death, but in fact it was not only my friend that appeared, but the clothes which he or she was wearing at the time, or the clothes to which I was accustomed. If the spirit was there in person, were his clothes also brought in spirit form?

The standard work on this subject is G. N. M. Tyrell's *Apparitions* (Duckworth, 1942). Out of the various possibilities, the most sensible seems to me to be basically telepathy: I become aware, through mind-to-mind contact at a deep level, of my friend's distress. This may remain as no more than a general uneasiness, but alternatively my conscious mind may clothe the awareness in a form or voice that becomes perceptible as a person in space.

This is sensible if we consider the phenomenon of hypnotism and post-hypnotic suggestion. Hypnotism has been grossly misused as a stunt. It is used far less nowadays, even in psychiatry. But if I were to hypnotize you, and you were a good subject, I might suggest to you that at 3 o'clock you would see your local Member of Parliament entering the room and sitting down in the chair next to you. He would talk to you about local reforms. Then at precisely 3 o'clock anyone else in the room would find you behaving as though all were happening as I had suggested. The M.P. would evidently appear to you, sit down, and talk to you.

Nobody understands how hypnotism works, but it is as if I implanted an idea in the depths of your mind, and your brain then fed it back in a reverse direction. Instead of the nerve impulses from exterior sense organs stimulating certain parts of the brain to produce sight and sound, these parts of the brain are stimulated from within so as to create the illusion that there really is a figure and a voice in the room. Incidentally, we call this figure an hallucination. To go back to the ghost, this also is an hallunication, but it may nevertheless be what is called a *veridical* hallucination if it coincides with some true situation or communication that the distant person is trying to create for you.

To return to Barrett's account: if one or more of the group had received the telepathic awareness of the death of their friend, Hugh Lane, the knowledge would emerge via the board. The fact that the communicator could not give information later about a codicil to his will, which was in dispute, makes one suspect that the real Hugh Lane was not present.

We note one point which Barrett does not raise at the time. He describes* the complete blindfolding of the group, including himself, and the shuffling of the letters of the alphabet, which were placed under glass. What happened then was that the small board on which the hands were resting 'rushed round and round as if polishing the glass, and then proceeded more slowly to inspect, as it were, each letter of the alphabet, going round each letter till all were located'.

The sitters were blindfolded. So let us ask a realistic question. Where were the 'spirit's' eyes? From the description it would sound as though they were on the pointer of the moving board. This of course is absurd. If on the other hand the spirit was aware of what was going on in the room, it would have been aware of the order of the letters without having to go round and inspect each one, unless spirits are shortsighted. If, however, we ask, how did Sir William Barrett know what the board did, and how did the blindfolded sitters know what words it spelt out, the answer must be that there was a person who was not blindfolded, and who was recording the movements of the board. If there was a spirit, it must have used his eyes to locate the

---

Proceedings of S.P.R., Vol. XXX, p. 243.

letters. But once the recorder knew the order of the letters, he could become the channel of the telepathic faculties of the group as a whole, and we need not postulate a spirit at all.

If group telepathy is all that is involved in the ouija board and the tumbler, it may sound very harmless. Before we discuss the dangers, we ought to look at the possibility that spirits are actually involved, remembering as we said earlier that it may not be an either/or but a both/and.

There are some lifelong investigators of spiritualistic phenomena who are convinced that all can be explained by fraud, or by telepathy and clairvoyance. If in place of *all* one puts *much*, this, I believe, is a fair estimate.

The average person who goes to a seance jumps a logical gap when he is told something that only he and the departed relative know, or is reminded of something that he did that morning before coming to the seance, or when he is told of some future event which does in fact come to pass. He concludes that these revelations are a proof that it is indeed his relative who has communicated. Yet the first two pieces of information are already available for mind-to-mind telepathy—his mind and the medium's. For the third he assumes that only a spirit can know the future. Spirits may or may not know the future, but it is certainly a fact, as Osty and others have demonstrated, that some human beings with the gift of second sight make unaided the same sort of prediction as the alleged spirit does.

9. PSYCHIC FORCE

WE have been considering some psychic capacities inherent in man as an explanation of the knowledge and error communicated by the ouija board and at the seance. We cannot leave the subject without exploring further reaches of the purely psychic. We must look at what is popularly called the influence of mind over matter.

Perhaps the simplest place to begin is with our own mind and body. It is difficult to define the term *mind*, but we can think of it as our capacity for building on what our physical senses supply. Some would prefer a tighter and more traditional definition, but, since there is so much dispute about it among the philosophers, we will try to make do with the more general statement.

A word which has emerged in recent times is *psychosomatic*. Medically this word indicates that it is often not enough to treat the body, since the illness, which is perfectly genuine, is promoted and kept alive by a disturbed inner attitude. Apart from illness, we all know how there is a constant two-way connection between attitude and bodily well-being or ill-being. Good news injects a healing psychic force, bad news an unhealthy one. This is the practical truth that underlies Christian Science. Our mind influences our matter.

If we look away from ourselves, we know that some people radiate an atmosphere of well-being, quite apart from things that they say and do. Many doctors have this additional healing touch. Moreover, there are people who have a natural gift of healing. Often they project healing through the laying-on of their hands. Some patients who have been helped by such healers as Agnes Sanford have been aware of a feeling of warmth passing into their body from her hands. Like every natural capacity, this gift should be put into the hands of God to use as He prompts, but only too often it becomes linked to spiritualism.

Since the middle of the last century experiments have apparently shown that some people could affect galvanometer needles and electroscopes by an act of will when they extended their hand towards them. Descriptions of these experiments are usefully summarized in Rene Sudre's *Treatise on Parapsychology* (Allen and Unwin) in the chapter headed *Psychic Fluid*, which is an equivalent name for what I am calling *Psychic Force*. Yet another name is *Odic* or *Odylic Force*. The word *Od* was coined by the Austrian chemist Reichenbach, about 1845, to describe a natural energy permeating the universe and emanating from a human being as animal magnetism.

At the time of writing this book, there are several experiments being conducted to demonstrate or refute the influence of mental concentration on living or material objects. At Duke University for some years Dr. J. B. Rhine and others have claimed that such concentration can affect the fall of dice, whether thrown by hand or mechanically. Thus, willing high numbers has produced a bigger run of high numbers than would be expected by chance, and willing low numbers has produced the opposite. Others have reported some slight success in willing creatures to move in one direction rather than another, or to one half of a microscope slide rather than the other. Some people claim to have moved small objects under glass. Others are investigating so-called 'green fingers' as influencing the health of plants. One new phenomenon is the production of photographs on unexposed films by Ted Serios in America. I am prejudiced against the genuineness of this, since I know how spirit photographs have been faked in the past. Yet after reading *The World of Ted Serios* by the researcher Jule Eisenbud, I am certainly impressed, since Serios produced good results under what seem to be cast-iron conditions. Spirit photography has gone out of vogue since films replaced plates. Plates could easily be doctored and switched. Films cannot be faked in the same way. But a psychic force that can create light to expose a photograph of an object that is not in the room, opens up yet another area of possibility to bewilder us.

If we admit the realm of psychic force, we can link it to the divining of water and other objects. The water diviner with his hazel twig or other 'instrument' has no conscious awareness of where the water flows, but the presence of the water makes itself felt by an uncontrollable movement of the twig. Since the twig does not move when separated from the diviner, it must be that he supplies the 'current' to a 'radar' twig, and this responds to a field of force that flows from the underground water. It twists when it comes nearest to the water, i.e. directly over it. Although diviners have sometimes failed completely under test, they have a sufficient run of success to make it worth the while of big companies to use them to discover water.

In discussing telepathy we concluded that mind can be in contact with mind at a deep level. Can this contact ever be used actively so that one mind exerts an influence on another? Witchcraft and magic work on the assumption that it can. They attempt to mobilize psychic force, although they often combine this with the invocation of supernatural beings. Witchcraft in one form or another has been practised down the ages. Certain men and women have inherited or developed powers of working spells. There is a description in Ezekiel 13. 17-23 of women who made use of magic wrist bands and veils to put death curses on certain people, and to give assurance of personal safety to others. This sort of thing is practised by witch doctors today. The majority of deaths that result are almost certainly due to auto-suggestion, since the victim is made aware of the curse by signs left on his doorstep. Similarly an amateur palmist at a local Bingo club told another member that he could not see any future for him in his hand. The man was dead in a fortnight, and I should judge it to be more than a 50 per cent chance that his death was due to auto-suggestion.

Where a curse is put on someone there may well be a direct psychic force in addition to the force of suggestion. Certainly missionaries have been aware of an unseen black force that has confronted them when the local witch doctor has mobilized his powers against the Gospel work. C. T. Studd once found himself unable to speak at a gathering in Africa, until by an effort he broke through in the Name of Christ. The witch doctors had gathered to silence him.

In his book, *Experiences of a Present Day Exorcist* (Wm. Kimber, London, 1970), Donald Omand gives two stories from his personal experience of occasions when little figures were plaited from straw to represent someone on whom a curse was to be placed. As the figure was pierced with pins, so the victim was taken ill. One case was probably due to suggestion, but in the other instance, where a healthy young Nazi died suddenly of angina, the victim had no knowledge of the figure that was hidden in his room with a pin buried in its 'heart'.

There is another form of witchcraft today which has had some publicity on T.V. and radio. There have been interviews with women who claim to be heads of covens, or groups of witches. The late curator of the Isle of Man folk museum, Gerald Gardner, wrote a book, *Witchcraft Today,* in which he claimed to be the head of a coven. He disowned all connection with Satanism, and such description as he was free to give of this form of witchcraft showed that it was a form of Nature worship, totally pagan, centring in a goddess like the

Babylonian Ishtar. Again, there is the manipulation of psychic force, and the coven, naked and oiled, join in a circle to generate power, which they then try to project for beneficial purposes.

To return to the other type of witchcraft, which crosses the border into black magic, this is often an occasion for every kind of sexual orgy. From time to time the papers print revelations, which may be touched up but which I am sure are basically true. Sometimes there is defiant Satanism. A Christian has the assurance from the Bible that God is ultimately in control, however much He allows freedom to Satan and to human beings. Jesus Christ has made the victory sure, as we saw in an earlier chapter. If one does not accept the Bible, one can gamble on the hypothesis that the God of the Christians is not as strong as He professes to be, and that with enough supporters Satan will eventually triumph. Looked at through purely human eyes, there is much in the world situation to support this.

Thus people turn to Satanism, and challenge God by desecrating objects that are used in Christian worship, such as the Communion bread (or wafer) and wine, and vestments and candles from churches. Parodies of Christian services and prayers are part and parcel of the ceremonies. Churchyards are desecrated, and occasionally there are suspected ritual murders. One doubts whether most of these gatherings generate much psychic force, but undoubtedly they form channels for the liberation of evil atmospheres into the world of today.

There is, however, a further world of straight magic. The Bible recognizes Egyptian magicians who produced comparable phenomena to what God produced through Moses and Aaron, though only up to a point. (Exodus 7. 10-12, 22; 8. 7, 18.) The most notorious of modern magicians was Aleister Crowley, who died in 1947. His books are still sold at a high price, but his moral behaviour and his defiance of God are appalling by any standards.

There are, however, other non-Christian magicians who regard moral strictness as necessary for their success. Indeed their pattern of development comes close to some forms of mysticism, as A. D. Duncan points out in *The Christ, Psychotherapy, and Magic* (Allen & Unwin, 1969), the difference being that 'The mystic seeks God. The magician seeks the things of God' (p. 50). The magician seeks such comprehension of his own union with the universal life-principle that he will have power to swim deliberately in the stream of creation, and, as part of the waters, to direct them—almost as God. We are back in the realm of psychic force, although on his way upward the magician may encounter, use, or subdue, lower and higher supernatural entities. In fact Colossians 2. 16-23 is most relevant, since it refers to the strict disciplines necessary in order to make contact with even angels and spirits, though Paul urges his readers not to do so, but to concentrate on Jesus Christ.

We postulate, then, a realm and activity of

psychic force, whereby, without introducing the intervention of spirit beings, some people can project an invisible influence beyond the reach of their physical senses. It may be that in turn they can receive an inflow from other individuals, and also from a force that permeates the universe. Physicists now know that the 'bricks' of the universe are not solid blocks, but mobile energy. This energy may be more than physical, and may somehow be related to the mind of man.

Then why should everyone not train himself to manipulate and be immersed in these energies? The answer seems to me to be a practical one. Those who cultivate them tend to become either bad, like black magicians, or power-inflated, like other magicians and witches, or pantheistic or atheistic, like practitioners of some forms of Yoga, who explore the personal and impersonal inner world without looking to God above.

As A. D. Duncan points out in *The Christ, Psychotherapy, and Magic,* the Christian who seeks a fuller awareness of God may find himself using certain techniques for stilling his racing thoughts, and for meditation, that can be paralleled by what occultists do, but his end and aim are entirely different. Thus, in learning from the methods of others, the Christian does not aim to become a manipulator of psychic force, since this would be to repeat the sin of eating from the tree of the knowledge of good and evil in the hope of becoming like God (Gen. 3. 5). If God wishes to use any man's latent psychic force, He will naturally do so. We only run into trouble when we try to manipulate it for ourselves. A few Christian mystics, for instance, have experienced strange physical phenomena, such as levitation, but these have been incidental and not sought in themselves. Cases are included in Fr. Herbert Thurston's two books, *The Physical Phenomena of Mysticism* (1952, Burns Oates) and *Surprising Mystics* (1955, Burns Oates).

We need not be afraid of meditation if it is properly directed. In fact, it should form part of a daily time of personal Bible reading and prayer. Its misuse is to allow the mind to go passive and accept whatever comes up from the depths, as with an LSD trip. Christian meditation is anchored to what God has revealed in Scripture. It might, for example, sit down before Christ as the Bread of life, the Water of life, or the Way; or it might soak in a verse from the daily Scripture portion. Generally we relate our meditation to union with God. Where Christians differ from, say, eastern mystics is that we do not meditate on union with an unknown, immanent God, but on a God who is known in and through Jesus Christ and His death on the Cross, and in the indwelling of the Holy Spirit. The heart of the matter is summed up in Ephesians 2. 18: 'Through Jesus Christ we have access in one Spirit to the Father'. Whatever techniques we use for quietening our mind and body, we aim at allowing the words of Scripture to come to life in our inner being, so that they can be translated into dynamic life.

WE have reached a line of division. Some would be happy to stop with the hypothesis that psychic force is an explanation of all occult phenomena. On the other hand, a number of Christians would jump straight into the view that evil spirits are at the bottom of everything. Here let me say that, even if natural psychism alone could be the explanation, it would not follow that all use of psychic gifts is harmless. We shall take up some reasons for this later, but meanwhile, from the purely practical point of view, it is worth reading the cases that Kurt Koch presents in his book, *Between Christ and Satan*. Dr. Koch is a German evangelical pastor, who has had a special mission to people who have been inwardly and outwardly attacked as a result of participating in occult practices. In many of his quoted cases the attacks have come after such apparently simple things as fortune-telling and reciting charms, as well as after direct involvement in trying to contact spirits.

However, we are now looking for evidence for direct spirit intervention, although we shall not rule out the likelihood that spirits can use the natural psychic forces already in man. Let us turn first to the Bible.

A Christian is bound to give serious consideration to what the Bible says about our communication with the spirit world, and one cannot deny that the Bible is emphatically against attempting it. Unfortunately the AV is not as clear as it might be, and, by its regular use of the term *familiar spirits*, it switches our mind away from mediumship to witchcraft.

What are familiar spirits? The first known occurrence of this term in English literature is in the Geneva Bible of 1560, a translation made by exiled Protestants during Queen Mary's reign. During the second half of the century there are many references to familiars as the demons in the form of animals that were given to a witch when she made a pact with the devil. *Familiar* comes from the Latin, and means *servant*. The familiar served the witch in magical spells, and then was rewarded by sucking blood from some spot on the witch's body. This account of familiars is almost entirely English and Scottish. They are not mentioned in Elizabeth's Statute against witchcraft in 1563, but the James I Statute of 1604 refers to any person who shall 'entertain, employ, feed, or reward any evil and wicked spirit to or for any intent or purpose'.

Evidence of the existence of these familiars was obtained by similar brutal psychological methods to those that have been used to extract political confessions in modern times. This worthless evidence was supplemented by the discovery of any wart or mole or other blemish on the body of the witch, since this mark would be regarded as the teat from which the familiar was fed.

The AV translators, thinking only of current witch trials, augmented the Geneva references to familiar spirits, with the result that, as Dr. Basil Atkinson says in his Commentary on Leviticus 19. 31, 'The mediaeval and early post-Reformation world completely misunderstood the meaning of the witchcraft referred to in the Bible . . . Not till the return of spiritism and mediumship in the 19th century did the world know experimentally the witchcraft of the Bible'.

This can be demonstrated from the use of words and phrases in Scripture, and their translation in the modern versions of the Bible. The very full list and discussion that follow are for those who want to study the full Biblical usage.

There are two special Hebrew words to be noted. (1) OB. The O is long, and the B is softened with an H so as to be pronounced almost as a V. This is always translated *familiar spirit* in the AV. (2) YIDDEONI, with the final O and I long. The AV always translates this as *wizard*. The precise meaning of OB is uncertain, but a similar word in Arabic means *to return*. The second word is almost certainly connected with the Hebrew verb *to know*. So far as usage goes, it appears that both words refer to a communicating spirit.

The main references are as follows, and for the sake of readers who do not know Hebrew endings, I shall form the plural by adding an English 's'. Lev. 19. 31. 'Do not turn to the *obs* and the *yiddeonis;* do not seek them out to be defiled by them'.

Lev. 20. 6. 'If a person turns to the *obs* and to the *yiddeonis*, prostituting himself to them, I will set my face against him, and will cut him off from among his people'.

Lev. 20. 27. 'A man or a woman who has an *ob* or a *yiddeoni* shall be put to death'.

Deut. 18. 10, 11. 'There shall not be found among you anyone who ... consults an *ob* and a *yiddeoni* and inquires of the dead'. This is in a list of evils practised by the Canaanites, and concludes, 'For these nations give heed to soothsayers and diviners; but as for you, the Lord your God has not allowed you to do so'.

1 Sam. 28. 3. 'Saul had put out the *obs* and the *yiddeonis* from the land'.

1 Sam. 28. 7. 'Find me a woman who is owner of an *ob*, that I may go and inquire of her ... There is a woman who is owner of an *ob* in Endor'.

1 Sam. 28. 8. 'Divine for me with an *ob* and bring up for me whomever I shall name to you'.

1 Chron. 10. 13, 14. 'Saul consulted an *ob* and asked guidance, and did not ask guidance of the Lord. Therefore the Lord slew him'.

2 Kings 21. 6. Among the list of Manasseh's sins is the fact that he used an *ob* and *yiddeonis* (N.B. the singular and plural. The corresponding passage in 2 Chron. 33. 6 has both words in the singular).

2 Kings 23. 24. Josiah 'put away the *obs* and the *yiddeonis*'.

Isaiah 8. 19, 20. 'When they say to you, "Consult the *obs* and the *yiddeonis* that chirp and mutter", should not a people consult their God? Should they consult the dead on behalf of the living? To the teaching and to the testimony'! Isaiah 29. 4. 'Then deep from the earth you shall speak, from low in the dust your words shall come, and (literally) shall be as an *ob* from the earth your voice, and your speech shall chirp (as in 8. 19) from the dust'.

A close look at these passages shows that *ob* and *yiddeoni* can normally be titles of communicating spirits. Since *ob* is occasionally used by itself, whereas *yiddeoni* is always linked with an *ob*, it would be sensible to regard the *ob* as the main control spirit and the *yiddeonis* as the other spirits called up by the control. Most mediums today appear to have one or two main controls of this kind.

The passages which might need the translation of *mediums* are those that speak of putting aways *obs* and *yiddeonis* (1 Sam. 28. 3 and 2 Kings 23. 24). The words for *put away* are different in these two passages, but the meaning is similar. Even here we can keep the original meaning, while recognizing that you do in fact put away spirits by putting away the mediums who are their channels of communication. So we need not quarrel with modern translations that use the term *mediums* here.

The allusion to the sound of the spirit's voice

in the Isaiah passages is interesting, since a change of voice characterizes the medium in trance. Isaiah 8. 19 has two descriptive words. That which is translated *chirp* is used of a bird in Isaiah 10. 14 and of a swallow in 38. 14. Its only other occurrence is the one we have seen, where it is used of a voice from the dead in 29. 4. The AV and RV and RSV include the crane with the swallow here, but there is some doubt about the correct text, and the NEB and Jerusalem keep the swallow only. Since it is used twice of birds, we can regard it as an onomatopoeic word. In Hebrew it is *tsaphaph*, reminding us of the English chiffchaff, a bird named from its two-note song. *Chirp* then is the high-pitched note of a bird.

Mutter (*hegah*, with both syllables long) is also said by the lexicon to be onomatopoeic. It is used of the growl of a lion (Isaiah 31. 4) and of the low cooing of a dove (Isaiah 38. 14) but also it is used of meditation in Joshua 1. 8 and several times in the Psalms. This is because much meditation was a low-voiced repetition of passages of Scripture.

You may have noticed in these references, that the two words that describe the voice of the spirit in Isaiah 8. 19 do in fact occur together in 38. 14 of the swallow and dove respectively. They thus describe a high pitch and a low pitch voice, even if the trumpeting crane is included with the swallow. Isaiah thus indicates that the voices that the spirits used were above or below the normal register of the mediums.

Whatever may be the precise rendering of any single passage, it is beyond doubt that the Old Testament bans any attempt to contact the departed. This is true of the Law, the Historical Books, and the Prophets. Is there the slightest sign that the New Testament lifts the ban?

I once had a public debate with a spiritualist minister about the Bible's verdict on Spiritualism. Unfortunately we hardly got to grips, since his main argument was that the early Church experienced the psychic phenomena of the modern seance, with inspired prophets, tongues, and healings, while my argument was that these have nothing to do with contacting the departed, which is the essence of Spiritualism, and which we are now considering. The only possible example in the Bible which could in any sense be called a seance is the Transfiguration, but the once-for-all experience on the top of a mountain is very different from repeated seances in darkened rooms. The disciples were not told to go and do likewise, as they were with other things that Jesus did.

If we argue from silence, we are arguing from significant silence. In two passages Paul deals with the attitude which living Christians should have towards their departed loved ones (1 Thessalonians 4. 13-18 and 1 Corinthians 15. 17-19). If the early Christians practised mediumship, Paul would inevitably have appealed to the communication which the living Christians could have with the departed in the Christian services. As it is, he comforts the mourners by reminding them that their relatives are in Christ, and that the proof of their survival and subsequent resurrection is the resurrection of Jesus Christ.

Spiritualists make great play with the command to test the spirits (1 John 4. 1). Later we shall consider the form of the test in 1 John 4. 1-3 and 1 Corinthians 12. 3, but meanwhile we notice that the point of the test is not to decide whether the communicator is a deceiving spirit or, say, your grandfather, but whether it is an evil spirit or the Holy Spirit of God. No one other than the Holy Spirit inspires a true prophet: communication from a departed Jew or Christian never enters into the picture. This distinguishes the prophet of God from a medium.

It is therefore absolutely undeniable that God in the Bible has put a total ban on our attempt to communicate through mediums. This would obviously include attempts at do-it-yourself mediumship with a tumbler or ouija board. There are at least three possible reasons for this.

1. The communications that come to the bereaved are simply drawn from them by telepathy and clairvoyance, as we have already seen to be likely. Thus they are unconsciously deceived.

2. The Bible is not interested in proving survival. In fact it may distract from the urgency of living the Christian life if we are led to believe, as seance messages suggest, that life beyond the grave goes on

much the same as this life, with eating, drinking, dressing up, concerts, and lectures. The Bible is concerned with eternal life in Christ, and the point of eternal life is not simply that one survives death, but that one enjoys life of a new quality, which links us to God Himself through receiving the living Lord Jesus Christ into the centre of our being. When Christ says, 'I came that they may have life, and have it abundantly' (John 10. 10), and 'I am the resurrection and the life' (John 11. 25), He does not mean that He came just to assure us that we all survive death. Eternal life is something that He gives to those who come to Him belongingly (John 10. 27-30). Thus the consolations of the seance may actually blind us to the Gospel of Jesus Christ.

3. There are some researchers who scorn the trivialities of the seance, but who try to discover from advanced spirits a philosophy of the universe. Communications come through well-educated mediums, sometimes using automatic writing. I have read a number of these communications, and it is clear why the Bible puts a ban on them. Without any exception that I have discovered, these communicators deny the Deity of Jesus Christ (except in the non-Biblical sense that we are all allegedly sons of God) and His atoning death. These are the unique facts of revealed Christianity, and, if they are abandoned, Christianity becomes just one of the several great religions of the world.

It is a timely warning to read the spiritualist records of the Rev. Stainton Moses, one of the great mediums of the last century, e.g. *Spirit Teachings,* and to see how the spirits drew him gradually from the basic Christian faith. The alternative offered by the spirits in these and similar communications are, a good moral code, an encouragement to strive upwards, an unknown God, and, according to some, a series of reincarnations. In other words, we must make a choice between the incisive New Testament Christian faith, by which Christians have always lived, and a form of Theosophy. If the one is right, the other is wrong. They represent rival approaches to the meaning of life.

It is worth noting that the Biblical tests for the genuineness of alleged spirit utterances turn on what is said about Jesus Christ. The test in 1 Corinthians 12. 2, 3 is a general one. 'No one speaking by the Spirit of God ever says "Jesus be cursed!" and no one can say "Jesus is Lord" except by the Holy Spirit'. Here are the two extremes, an utter rejection of Jesus and a declaration of the highest honour possible. Since the word translated *Lord* is used in the Greek translation of the Old Testament as an equivalent of Jehovah or Yahweh, the context here suggests that it has the meaning of *Lord God,* as in John 20. 28 and Philippians 2. 11, although admittedly it can bear a lesser meaning.

The other test in 1 John 4. 1-3 has only recently come home to me in the light of the theosophical type of teaching to which I have referred. 'By this you know the Spirit of God: every spirit which confesses that Jesus Christ has come in the flesh is of God, and every spirit which does not confess Jesus is not of God. This is the spirit of antichrist'.

The teachings of Higher Thought commonly speak of the Christ within every man, and hold that the man Jesus was fully possessed by the Christ. This same view was held by some people in John's day. Thus the force of the test is the full incarnation of Jesus Christ, in contrast to the coming of the Christ into Jesus. When I was taking students in a study of some of the writings of the early fathers, I found to my surprise that some manuscripts had a different text in verse 3, 'Every spirit who looses Jesus is not of God', i.e. who splits Jesus from the Christ. This reading is included in the RV margin as 'annulleth Jesus'. The weight of manuscript evidence is against it, but at least it shows how early Christians interpreted the force of the words.

It seems reasonable to link this passage with 1 John 5. 6. 'This is He who came by water and blood, Jesus Christ, not with the water only but with the water and the blood'. Most commentators understand water to refer to the water of His baptism in the Jordan, when Jesus was designated as the Messiah (Christ). The heresy that John is excluding is the heresy that at this point the Christ descended on the man Jesus, and that this constituted the 'incarnation'. Christians saw, quite rightly, that this would not be a genuine incarnation, but an intensification of what the prophets experienced, namely a filling with the power or Spirit of God.

Commentators hold that the *blood* has reference to the atoning death of Christ, and it seems as though some also held that the Christ withdrew again from the man Jesus before the crucifixion. My own suggestion is that the *blood* here refers to the birth, as in John 1. 13. John there refers to Christians as being born of God, 'not of blood, nor of the will of the flesh, nor of the will of man', i.e. the three expressions describe natural birth. Therefore, since the heresy in 1 John certainly concerned the true incarnation of Jesus Christ, it seems likely that the meaning of the water and the blood is that the Sonship of Jesus Christ is not only the Messianic Sonship announced at His baptism, as He entered on His Messianic mission, but also the coming of the Son of God through the channel of human birth, a true incarnation.

The following minor points of the Greek text may be mentioned, although they do not affect this interpretation. The Greek in John 1. 13 is literally, 'not out of bloods'. We also speak of *blood relationship,* and Aristotle in the 4th century B.C. spoke of conception as coming through the mingling of a form of blood in the woman with a form of blood from the man. Thus in either case John means that the Christian new birth is not through the action of the parents. This is the same distinction as Christ makes in John 3. 6, 'That which is born of the flesh is flesh, and that which is born of the Spirit is spirit'.

In 1 John 5. 6 two prepositions are used. The

RSV and Jerusalem translate them as *by* and *with*, the NEB as *with* and *by*—which indicates that there is no great difference between them! Both His baptism and His birth were significant agents of His coming.

This excursion into the Greek has been important to establish the nature of the test that must be applied to the spirits when they communicate messages. They are not tests to be given to enquire into the medium's private beliefs. In every case that I have heard of where an instructed Christian put the test, the spirit has refused to admit the Deity of Jesus Christ and His true incarnation, and has made an end of the seance. These tests are rare, since instructed Christians do not usually attend these seances. If they do, their presence often inhibits any communication at all. In the only private seance that I attended, with a view to the writing that I was doing on spiritualism, we sat for some 45 minutes without any communications, and the medium commented that the spirits were slow in coming through. The communications that eventually came bore all the marks of being faked. Two well-known ministers were addressed by their 'mother' and by a 'former colleague' respectively, but neither spirit was able to give the affectionate names by which they had been known on earth. The names given were those that the medium could have discovered from books and writings beforehand. 'Unknowns' like myself did not receive any messages!

Similarly a vicar writes about his experiences

at a party when he was at College and was a nominal Christian. A table-tipping session was planned, but no one was obliged to take part. My correspondent says that he sat in an armchair and pretended to be asleep, but prayed hard that nothing would happen. Although the lady who arranged a similar party annually was experienced in seances of table-tipping, nothing occurred, and eventually she gave up, after announcing that there was someone in the room who did not believe. Another student, who also is now ordained, broke up by his presence a seance in an Indian temple, when he stood behind a pillar and prayed silently in the Name of Christ.

WE can begin to see reasons why the Bible clamps down absolutely on attempts to consult spirits. Either we receive what are no more than messages from our own hearts by telepathic awareness and psychometry, or, if we are interested in obtaining descriptions of conditions in the next world, or religious and philosophical information, the communications turn out to be cleverly-twisted attacks on the uniqueness of the Christian revelation. Jesus Christ may be given the exalted position that Satan offered Him in the wilderness temptations and that He refused (Matt. 4. 8-11); but He is not given the supreme position that His Father gave Him as the only Son, truly God, who became Man, and triumphed on the cross and in His resurrection and exaltation (Phil. 2. 5-11). He is not the Christ whom John saw in heaven (Rev. 1 and 5). One must make the choice between Jesus Christ as He gives Himself to us in the New Testament and the vague teachings of the clever spirit communicators.

In this chapter we want to discover other possible spirit manifestations, and also see how spirits can influence us from within. A good place to begin is with poltergeists, a German word meaning *noisy spirits*. In his book *Between Christ and Satan*, Dr. Kurt Koch, whom we have already mentioned, has been badly served by his translator. The good German *poltergeist* has been rendered *spook*, which, so far as I know, is never used of poltergeists, but is just a word of schoolboy and schoolgirl fun to describe an 'ordinary' ghost. We have regarded some hauntings as the result of imprints. These are the hauntings where material objects are not moved, but everything after the appearance is as it was before. But poltergeists move things, and the noise that they make is usually the banging of the objects they displace.

Certainly one must eliminate some of the reported cases of poltergeists, since they have turned out to be cleverly-staged frauds by children, or sometimes vibration caused by underground streams or by traffic, or rats or mice in the walls. Yet, when such cases have been eliminated, it is significant that similar phenomena have been recorded independently down the centuries from all parts of the world. Hereward Carrington in *The Invisible World* (Rider) mentions his analysis of some 320 cases between A.D. 530 and 1935, of which he finds 278 that cannot be explained by natural laws.

Harry Price in *Poltergeist over England* records even more. They occur, he finds, regularly in highly civilized countries as well as in primitive communities. Very similar things happen in each case. Furniture and other household objects are moved about; crockery and stones are thrown, sometimes in slow motion or round corners; occasionally bed-clothes are pulled off and the beds are shaken or even tipped up; sometimes fires are started. It is rare for any occupant of the house to be injured, although, in a recent case reported to me by a vicar, a hot water bottle flew through the air and hit the father of the house.

One example that must interest Christians is the poltergeist in the Wesley household when John Wesley's father was rector of Epworth. Southey reproduces the descriptive accounts and letters relating to this in an appendix to his *Life of Wesley*. The household was disturbed night and day by noises, the tramping of feet and the shaking of crockery and beds, although nothing was actually moved out of place. During family prayers the noises were particularly obstreperous in the prayers for the royal family. The children referred to the entity as Old Jeffery.

It was noticed that little Hetty Wesley was twitching in her sleep, sometimes shortly before the onset of the noises. This ties up with other poltergeist manifestations where there is someone who seems to be at the centre of the manifestations. This may be a child, an unmarried teenager, or an older person who is passing through a time of mental stress. In fact one can make a case for poltergeist phenomena being a breakdown outside the body. If so, we are back at our theory of psychic force. It may be, yet almost certainly this bursting energy is in this case being taken up and directed by a spirit entity. The proof of this is that a poltergeist is usually exorcised by prayer and command in the Name of Christ. Both the invisible spirit and the rooms in the house are 'cleansed' in this way, although naturally the person through whom the force is being drawn may need counselling and help to solve the repressed problems which are creating the energy.

A vicar recently sent me a report of a difficult case in which he, as well as the family, had experienced frightening noises and the movement of objects and furniture. He also sent me a tape recording of an interview with the family afterwards. Since the report was confidential, I cannot give any details that might identify the parish or family. At first prayer and attempts at cleansing had no effect, and the phenomena grew more intense. They ceased for a time after further prayer, and then returned. There was a most unusual ending to the story, in that the spirit apologized to the family, and asked for prayer. They asked whether it wanted to go to Jesus, and it replied that it did, and, after the family had prayed intensely for some minutes, they were conscious of a lifting of the atmosphere, and the spirit left them. The change was also felt by the dog, which previously had been uneasy and restless, and had refused to go upstairs. Similarly the Wesleys' dog appeared to sense the presence of Old Jeffery.

In this case there were three significant facts. A young man in the house appeared to be the centre from which some force was drawn. Also, the daughter had been badly upset by dabbling in spiritualism two years ago. There had been a suicide some time previously in the house next door, which was at this time being demolished. Incidentally the spirit named itself to the girl before departing, giving the same name as a spirit had given when she was practising spiritualism; incidentally she did not divulge what the name was.

A Christian lady has sent me a newspaper report of a poltergeist case that happened in a vicarage near Malvern, in 1952. She vouches for the truth of it, since she and several other Christians went to assist the vicar and curate in prayer, but once again it was a battle of weeks before the disturbances ceased. In this case the vicar was repeatedly thrown out of bed; he and his sceptical churchwarden saw a heavy chest moved; bells rang, and there were weird howling noises.

A curate sent me a report of a case which was passed to the Society for Psychical Research. He was called in when a family found things being moved and rearranged in an attic room. The husband saw a broom, which he had carried upstairs, lift itself up and travel across the room. In this case their young daughter was a nervous and sensitive type of girl, and the wife suffered from depression. On a later occasion the curate and a doctor, who were spending a night in the house, saw her walking in her sleep and moving objects about, so undoubtedly she could have been physically responsible for some of the phenomena. At other times the wife was with her husband when things were moved, but her disturbed state may have produced the psychic force on these occasions. It may also be relevant that the husband's aunt had died a fortnight before the troubles first began.

I have several times had long talks with Dom

Robert Petitpierre, an Anglican monk who has had a vast amount of experience in practical encounters with the powers of evil. In a privately printed leaflet on exorcism he has a section on the exorcism of places, and includes the following phenomena as predisposing causes that can be linked to evil spirits:

(*a*) Poltergeist activity due to psychic action from some uncontrolled human subconsciousness, or to the influence of magicians, or perhaps to some non-human, mischievous sprite.

(*b*) Haunts deliberately created by black magicians.

(*c*) Demonic interference, often arising from habitual seances, but sometimes occurring on Christian sites that have been desecrated, or on ancient sites of pagan magic. There is some evidence that lines of force still exist, linking pagan magic centres together across the country, and magicians are now endeavouring to use them. Another clergyman, who has had some most unpleasant experiences in dealing with haunts, confirmed this from his own experience.

(*d*) Human sin, i.e. a place of bad sexual behaviour, occasionally an old fertility cult, or a place of business devoted to greed or domination, since human sin opens the door for other evil forces to enter.

I myself would be inclined to add the habitual use of drugs. Since the modern craze for mind-releasing drugs has still to run its course, we should keep our eyes open for the possible stepping-in of evil spirits when the God-given safeguard of conscious intelligence is broken down.

In this book I have confined myself mostly to

examples from Britain, but a recent conversation with a Christian leader from Kenya is worth including here. His father was the first convert from his village, and returned there as preacher and teacher. Gradually a Church was gathered in the face of much opposition. There was a well on the edge of the forest, and this and the surrounding forest were haunted by spirits, who spoke to many of the people when they went to draw water. After the Church was built, the spirits retreated, and told the people before they left that it was the ringing of the Church bell morning and evening that was driving them away. No doubt spirits could stand a bit of noise, but it was the Christian significance of the bell that drove them out, as it called Christians to pray. The fact remains that neither Christians nor pagans heard the spirit voices any longer.

In addition to possession of places, we must consider possession of individuals by evil spirits. Again, Christian ministers who are used to exorcism recognize these, but modern thought is suspicious of the concept of demon possession. A standard work in support of the belief is the rare work by Dr. J. L. Nevius, *Demon Possession and Allied Themes* (1892), written from experiences in China. The tendency today is to regard all the phenomena as psychological in origin. Yet Jesus Christ believed in it, and distinguished between normal illnesses, to be cured by laying-on of hands or anointing, and demon-possession, to be cured by the word of command (e.g. Matt. 10. 8; Mark 6. 13; Luke 13. 32). Any practising psychologist who could cure 'an extensive complex of compulsive phenomena'—as such possession has been called—by a word of command would soon be a rich man, and would clear up the waiting lists that are the nightmare of psychiatry.

If full possession is rare in this country, obsessive attacks by spirits are likely to be met with, particularly among those who have been mixed up with the occult. In preparing this book I have been sent tragic reports of students and others who have suffered in this way. Thus one clergyman writes of four students who after one or two seances 'were depressed, suicidal, and subject to compulsive behaviour', which included being forced to stop and stand outside certain houses. Two other girls were urged to commit suicide by spirits alleged to be their fathers, and one attempted it. In *Viewpoint* 16 (Autumn 1970) there is a vivid account of a boy in a house party who went rigid at the suggestion of a seance, and was restored only by commanding prayer. He had previously been inwardly attacked at an earlier seance.

How do these spirits get a footing in a human being? They obviously come in via the Unconscious, and probably through the function that we call the spirit. This seems to be the way of exit and entrance for the spirit world. It is intended to be the life link with the Holy Spirit of God, but, if it is unoccupied by Him, it can be the entrance for an evil spirit. Since man is a unity, entry here can influence any part or all parts of the personality.

Normally a human being is a defended castle, but any trafficking with the spirit world lets down the drawbridge. Once the bridge is down, it is extremely difficult to close it again by an act of will. Jesus Christ, who of course understood these things, told of the danger for anyone who has had an evil spirit driven out of him. If he merely tries to keep the house of his life clean but empty, the spirit may return with others beside (Luke 11. 24-26). In the previous verses Christ had led up to this diagnosis by presenting Himself as the one stronger than Satan, who comes to occupy the palace that Satan had possessed.

I think also that deliberate sins can open the door to spirit influence, in the sense that a spirit may fasten on your habits and drive you into some evil behaviour, and perhaps force you into a breakdown. Here the disentangling from sin through Jesus Christ may itself break the spirit's grip, and even psychiatric treatment by breaking the habit could weaken the spirit's influence, though without dealing with the root cause.

Several times we have adopted hypotheses to guide our thinking in the light of Scripture and experience. My own theory of spirit-control is, to the best of my knowledge, not taken from anyone else, but it is worth considering. One of the strange things that we touched on briefly is hypnotism. No one knows how it works, but the hypnotic suggestion clearly touches a control centre, which then puts it into action. The suggestion may be to do something, say something, or be something. If a spirit can reach this centre, he can plant the suggestion that will then be worked out. Obviously spirits cannot do this just as they please, they must first be let in by invitation, as with the ouija board, or by some persistent sin. The occult, with its direct appeal, seems to be the most usual occasion of entry. From the hypnotic centre the spirit can induce visions, voices, and compulsions. Since these so frequently follow dabbling in the occult, it is obvious that the spirits that one seems to contact—father, mother, husband, wife—are not what they seem to be, since they would not cause these after-effects. Most of these spirits are content with obsession (a kind of haunting), getting malicious satisfaction out of upsetting their victim. Occasionally they can implant a major controlling idea that changes the whole personality, and, since they are now riding the victim, they produce what is called demon-possession. In this they get the satisfaction of using the body by a semi-incarnation.

If we ask why they do not always go to the limit, the Scriptural answer is probably found in Job 1. 12 and Luke 22. 31, 32, where Satan has a limit imposed by God beyond which he cannot go when he is allowed to affect human lives. So the mercy of God curbs the power of individual attacks on the control centre, even though He has made man so that any emptiness of spirit is a tacit invitation to attack and invasion (cf. Matt. 12. 43-45), and any direct approach to the spirit world is the exercise of man's free choice to invite the spirits to come in. The vital thing is that obsession and possession are facts, whether or not the analogy with hypnotism is worth following up.

Vic Ramsey of New Life Foundation writes in *Viewpoint 16,* 'From our own experience over the past six years we have witnessed a serious interest in the occult among drug takers.' It is likely that these drugs can act as an opener up for evil spirits to come in at a deep level, since drugs, apart from being evil in themselves, lower the God-given barriers that consciousness sets up. Certainly the initiation of many shamans and witch doctors, leading to deliberate possession, is assisted by drugs. I personally wonder how much addictive craving is then produced by evil spirits, so that they can share physical and emotional experiences that are otherwise denied to them. One might compare the way sexually inhibited humans look for vicarious, yet shared, satisfaction through pornographic pictures and books.

Someone who is competent to do it might well investigate the effect of some rhythms and music for good or bad. Like every gift of God, music has its uplift and its degradation. Just as drugs can induce possession, so certain rhythms and drummings can do the same. Voodoo is an excellent example, and there is no better book on the subject than Maya Deren's *Divine Horsemen* (Thames and Hudson, 1953). Maya Deren went as a student of Haitian religion, and ended by getting 'hooked' herself.

One is often asked whether a Christian can

become possessed. Missionaries who are familiar with possession tell how converts have burned their idols and charms after having had evil spirits cast out of their bodies. Destruction by burning is important, since the idols definitely absorb evil. If the converts have later returned to idol worship, they have again become possessed. Christians in this country who before conversion have been involved in magic have had spiritual, psychic, and physical battering after conversion. They have been threatened by spells from former colleagues, and have had to call on other Christians to fight in prayer to keep the door closed to spirit interference. Any Christian who at any time opens up the door to spirits is in danger of being disturbed by them afterwards. He has done something that cannot simply be shrugged off and forgotten. However, experience suggests that this disturbance is more likely to follow several contacts than a single attempt, which may be made quite innocently. No one who has read this book could now dabble innocently.

The Bible shows that God brings or allows some punishments in order to recall His people to their senses. This, for example, is the Biblical interpretation of the exile in Babylon. So, although we cannot escape the defiance of spiritual laws any more than physical, God can temper them for our good. If I lay myself open to spirit invasion, I shall very likely have disturbing and frightening experiences, but, if I have previously known the power of God in my life, I may see what I am doing and quickly turn back to Him in confession, and ask Him to throw back the spirits and close the gate. If I persist with the spirits, I shall be in much more serious danger.

12. DO THE DEPARTED RETURN?

In writing about spirits, we have kept almost entirely to evil spirits, or demons, and said little about departed human spirits. In this chapter we want to go further, and consider the evidence for returning human spirits. This means first having a look at the Biblical revelation about the present state of the departed.

One of the most remarkable *non sequiturs* of spiritualism, even of spiritualism held by members of the Christian Churches, is that there is no universal Day of Judgement and no Resurrection of the body. It is said that all spirits are judged at death and have a soul-body and spirit-body in which to express themselves. The *non sequitur* comes from the fact that the Day of Judgement and the general Resurrection are always linked to the Second Coming of Christ according to the Bible, and Christ has not yet come. So, if the spirits have actually communicated and described their experiences *up to now*, they, like us, still stand on this side of the Second Coming, and cannot argue that there will be no Judgement and no Resurrection when this occurs!

There is a further lack of bite in the spiritualists' argument. They claim to have proved the fact of life after death through communications from the departed. Again, assuming the communications to be genuine, all that they prove is that some individuals, or some parts of them, have persisted for a time beyond the grave. In his book *The Supreme*

Adventure (James Clarke) Robert Crookall asserts that, as spirits go on to higher spheres, they can no longer make direct communication through mediums (p. 228). It would be equally possible to argue that they cease to communicate because they have disintegrated.

So we must remind ourselves that we are dealing with what is often called the Intermediate State, the present state of the departed person between death and the return of Christ. The Bible has little to say about this, but what it does say is significant. The Christian departs 'to be with Christ' (Phil. 1. 23). When he is absent from the body, he is 'at home with the Lord' (2 Cor. 5. 8). This presence with the Lord is in marked contrast with the communications that come through mediums, in which God and Christ are incidentals, if they are mentioned at all. The message that Bishop Pike recorded in his book, *The Other Side*, as coming from his son, is typical: 'They talk about Jesus—a mystic, a seer. Oh, but Dad, they don't talk about Him as a saviour.' One contrasts this with Revelation 5. 6-14.

The spiritualist's description is of something like a well-supplied holiday camp. Evidently these communicators have missed the Christian sphere, and, because I judge from the lives of some of them that they were Christians, I doubt whether they themselves are communicating, especially if, as often happens, they now attack the Christian faith.

The Bible admits that in the intermediate state a human being is incomplete. A human being, as planned and created by God, is a body-being. This does not mean that the person cannot exist without a body, but without a body he is not the full human being that God created. Paul describes this state as being without clothes. In 2 Corinthians 5. 1-10 he says that he is well aware that there is an eternal heavenly body awaiting him (v. 1). He longs to be alive at the Second Coming of Christ, because then he would receive his new body at once, without passing through an intermediate period of nakedness (vs. 2-4). However, he takes comfort in the fact that, even without the body, he will be at home with the Lord (vs. 6-8), and he continues to live in the realization that he will one day stand before the judgement seat of Christ (vs. 9, 10).

Man must once again become fully man, or death will have had the last word. The idea of bodily resurrection has its difficulties, but we may approach it like this. First, the risen body of Jesus Christ is the pattern. This is argued in 1 Corinthians 15, and it is stated specifically in Philippians 3. 21 that Christ will change our bodies to be like His.

Secondly, if an essential part of man is destroyed by death, then death has conquered, and since death is the result of original and personal sin, there will be a permanent monument to sin in the existence of maimed human beings. Thus 1 Corinthians 15. 26 speaks of death as the last enemy to be destroyed: the resurrection destroys him.

A third point needs careful thinking. In this life our body is an expression of ourselves. Inner character changes outward appearance. Before conversion a person may have a degraded look. Almost immediately afterwards his whole face and bearing change. A new directing YOU, empowered by the Holy Spirit, has used your intake of food and air to mould a new body, which may well become far healthier than the old. At death YOU can no longer build the body that you have left behind. But as a Christian you are not without the means of expression and joy, since you are still linked to Christ by the Holy Spirit. But you are still unclothed. At the Resurrection you will be given the capacity to draw to yourself all that is needed to express yourself in a body. On earth you were limited in the extent to which you could form your body after the pattern of Christ. Now, because of the Holy Spirit within, you form an expression of yourself that is recognizably you, but is also YOU after the likeness of Christ.

On the other hand the person who is without Christ lacks the life link during the intermediate state. He had learnt only how to express himself in a body. Those who, like Dives, the rich man in Luke 16. 19-31, have lived only to indulge the body, now are scorched with the flame of unsatisfied desire (v. 24). When the opportunity comes to express themselves once again in a body, since there is a resurrection also of the lost (John 5. 29), there is no joint creative work with the Holy Spirit, but only a replica of what they were on earth.

We cannot presume to sift the wheat from the tares, nor to say how God judges those who have never been confronted with the call of Christ, but the story of Dives and Lazarus must be very relevant when it speaks of the impassable chasm between the saved and the lost in Hades, the intermediate state (vs. 23, 26).

Do we go to heaven when we die? Yes and No. Heaven is where Christ is, and in one sense even on earth we are 'in the heavenly places in Christ Jesus' (Eph. 2. 6). Whether or not we call the intermediate state *Hades*, with *Paradise* as the sphere of the saved (Luke 23. 43), it is where Christ radiates His presence in a fuller way than we have known on earth (Phil. 1. 23). But there is a new heaven and a new earth to come (Rev. 21 and 22) and our new bodies will be adapted for whatever conditions these may bring. Here there will be the opportunity for wholly God-centred service in the radiating glory of the Trinity (Rev. 22. 3-5).

After all this necessary consideration of the present state of the departed, we come back to our original question of whether departed spirits can return. Omitting those who were temporarily restored to life again, the Bible shows that they have done so on two occasions. The first is when Samuel came back to tell Saul that he would fall in battle next day (1 Samuel 28). Some interpreters think that this was not a genuine appearance of Samuel, but a counterfeit called up by the medium. However, the form of the story implies that the medium was taken aback at the appearance of Samuel. This was not the sort of spirit she was accustomed to raise.

Incidentally Samuel was distressed at being brought back (v. 15), unlike spirits raised today, who seem anxious to communicate.

The other return was on the Mount of Transfiguration, when Moses and Elijah conversed with Christ (Matt. 17. 3). Allowing for the fact that Elijah did not die in the normal way (2 Kings 2. 11), God deliberately planned for these two representatives of the Law and the Prophets to come back and talk with the Messiah about His coming death, which had been the theme of the Law and the Prophets (Luke 9. 31 and 24. 27).

These two single examples, which include no encouragement to secure their repetition, do not justify modern attempts to bring the departed back to the seance room. There are, however, many cases of the spontaneous appearance of loved ones around the time of their death, without any intervention by mediums. Moreover, there is no reason why God should not for His own purposes allow a spirit to return. In the story of Dives and Lazarus, Abraham did not say that it was impossible for Lazarus to return to earth, but that it would be useless for him to try to influence Dives' brothers if he did return (Luke 16. 27-31).

One story that always seems to me to be genuine is the Chaffin Will case. James Chaffin died in North Carolina in 1921. His only known will had been made in 1905, and by it he left all his property to his third son. The will was proved, but the son died about a year after inheriting. In 1925 the second son had several visions of his father, dressed in his old black overcoat. On one occasion the father said 'You will find my will in my overcoat pocket'. The elder brother had the overcoat, but in a sewn-up inner pocket there was a paper saying, 'Read the 27th Chapter of Genesis in my daddie's old Bible'. The Bible was in a drawer, and between the pages where Genesis 27 was printed there was another will made in 1919 by which the father divided his property equally between his four sons. This would seem to be a spontaneous communication from Chaffin himself, and no medium was involved.

There is nothing in Scripture to suggest that the departed are all around us and watching what we are doing. Samuel, Moses, and Elijah had certain specific knowledge, as we have seen; but all three on earth had had the gift of prophecy, which was something over and above their natural perception. It involved receiving direct communication from God. If God sent them back on a special mission, He told them what they needed to know, and there is no evidence that they picked up their knowledge from observation of what was passing on earth.

In this context, one of the most misapplied verses is Hebrews 12. 1, where 'the cloud of witnesses' is interpreted as a crowd of spectators. The word *witness* in English has this ambiguity, but the NEB sensibly makes the meaning clear by translating, 'With all these witnesses to faith around us like a cloud', thus referring us back to chapter 11, to the examples of faithful testimony (*witness*) even to death that we must ever keep before our eyes. In fact, the Greek word for *witness* is identical with the English *martyr*.

We cannot tell, then, whether the departed know what we are doing, and it is unlikely that they are wandering invisibly around the world. Since Christians are 'in Christ' both in life and death, Christ forms the ground of union between us all, and, as occasion arises, our loved ones may be aware through Him of some of the joys and sorrows through which we are passing. They may be told when someone they have loved is about to join them, for there are examples of deathbed visions when the one who is dying speaks of the presence of loved ones who have passed on.

13. WHAT SHOULD I DO?

THE purpose of this book has been to give a Christian interpretation of a subject that is attracting very much interest at the present time. Many readers will not be personally involved in the occult, and will be happy to stay that way. But for others the subject is far more immediately relevant, since they or their friends have been or could be involved in some way. What should they do about it?

I say 'could be', so that we can start now to beware of even beginning. Do not attempt to make any contact with any spirits, whether through mediums, ouija boards, sliding tumblers, automatic writing, or magic. If you do, you are deliberately trying something upon which God has put an invariable ban in Scripture. And please do not be caught by the argument that other things are forbidden in the Old Testament that Christians allow today, such as eating bacon. If communications with the departed were of benefit to them or to us, they would be so important that the New Testament at least would have lifted the Old Testament ban and encouraged us to help one another in this way. But although it modifies some of the social regulations of the Old Testament, the New Testament never withdraws the ban on contacting spirits.

We are not being narrow and obstructive. In these days there is hardly one Biblical command that is not challenged. God's word about fornication and adultery is being disputed even by writers who profess the Christian standpoint. Many of our accepted standards have dropped to the levels of Greece and Rome. The punishment that must follow as an inevitable result is the decay of both individual and society. It is God's punishment, but it is not arbitrary. Experimental spirit contact is as inevitably disastrous as experimental sex. In both cases what the Bible says is borne out by what experience demonstrates.

In this book we have distinguished between contacting the spirits from our side, and accepting occasional unsought, and generally unrepeated, appearances of a loved one around the time of their death. When Jesus Christ appeared to His disciples after His resurrection, they thought He was a ghost. Jesus did not reply that there were no such things as ghosts, but said that 'no ghost has flesh and bones as you can see that I have' (Luke 24. 39, NEB). If your friend appears to you, he is out of the body. When Jesus appeared, He was in the body, although, when His body rose from the grave, it was transformed so as to have new properties that it did not have before.

What are we to say about second sight in general? We are on more difficult ground here, and Christians are divided over our attitude to it. Since I have been writing this book, I have found several Christians who have this gift occasionally, and who have been relieved to find me talking about it naturally. On the other hand an experienced Christian minister, who made valuable suggestions when he read this book in manuscript, is emphatic that a Christian should pray for the faculty to be removed. A Christian, whose mother had second sight, told me that she found it worrying. Obviously the proper thing is to pray that, if the 'gift' is not according to the will of God, He will take it away. If then it persists, we take it that He will use it if it is put into His hands.

A danger is that a spiritualist will sense that you have this gift, and will urge you to develop it in spiritualist circles. Obviously this is wrong. Or you could be tempted to develop it yourself by crystal gazing, or take up some form of fortune telling. Why would this be wrong? Because you do not become more useful to God, yourself, or your fellow humans by trying to foretell the future, which is what developing second sight leads to even when it does not deliberately invoke spirits.

Second sight may be thought of as presenting dangers similar to those of the gift of sex, in the modern rather restricted sense of the word. The joy of sex is a vital part of marriage, but, when sex is developed as a thing in itself, it becomes degrading and shabby, and slides into mere smut. Similarly, second sight, even in its mildest forms, is an ingredient of life that God can use only as we go straight ahead with Him. Its cultivation for its own sake leads to bypaths, and may spoil our inner and outer life.

Although the average person wants to use those who have second sight for foretelling the future, we feel wary of doing so for ourself or others; these desires should be turned into prayer, just as we pray when a friend tells us of some need in a letter. If we have a tendency to pick up atmospheres as a general sensation or in picture form, we shall be more sensitive to hauntings, but we will also be quicker to detect the inner needs of people whom we meet. I will not go further into this, but some readers will know the sort of things that I mean. I repeat again that I do not have these experiences myself.

A gift like water divining has no connection with spirits, and I see no reason why it should not be used for the good of mankind. It is probably an unusual, but natural, sensitivity to radiations.

Since I have suggested that some of the communications from mediums and the ouija board are telepathic and clairvoyant in origin, it may be argued that these do not come under the Biblical ban. Let us be clear about one basic fact, that those who use these means are testing to see whether they can contact spirits. They are not wanting to draw on the unconscious minds of themselves and the other participants. Suppose that what emerges is the product of their own minds, they are still being deceived by the apparent source of the messages in the spirit world. Experience shows that what emerges soon becomes a conglomeration of evil, even if it starts apparently harmlessly. I do not want to break down God-given barriers and allow a group evil to flow in and out, as it must do if a telepathic linkage is opened up.

This emergence of evil was brought home to me recently at a university conference when I was asked to speak on 'The Realm of the Psychic'. In conversations afterwards with agnostics as well as Christians, everyone who spoke to me told of the degrading effect that these practices had had on their acquaintances. No one defended them. It would seem that the entity which communicates could be understood as a personalization of everybody's evil, which can then flow back into individuals, leaving them worse than before. But in fact one must return to the both/and rather than the either/or. If evil spirits exist, they will make use of the dropping of the barriers, and take up and use the latent psychic capacities in those who have invited them in.

What if we have already been involved ourselves, or want to help those who have been involved and who come to ask us for help? For ourselves, we must ask for prayer from our Christian friends, and claim the victory of Christ for the whole of our being.

Apart from what we have done ourselves, we may from time to time have to face some unpleasant manifestation of the occult. On several occasions members of Christian Unions have encountered the results of seances in their colleges or halls of residence. These results may take the form of a well-defined sense of evil in some of the rooms and passages. Since non-Christian students have been responsible for letting these powers loose, it has seemed reasonable to suggest that Christian students should prove the power of Christ as stronger. Members of the

Christian Union have mobilized effective prayer, and Christ through them has removed the haunting. Naturally if the seances continue, the trouble will come again, but sometimes discerning Christians have broken up the communications by holding a prayer meeting at the time when a seance is being held.

Ministers are asked to help in unusual cases, and can usually put people in touch with someone who is experienced in dealing with occult manifestations, and whose gift is that of 1 Cor. 12. 10, 'the ability to distinguish between spirits', coupled with the capacity to deal with them by exorcism or other means.

Yet one must remember that it is not the superior magic of the exorcist, but the power of Christ that overcomes the spirit, and ministers have told me of how God has used them in exorcism without any special gifts; they have simply acted according to Scripture. Some exorcists use adaptations of traditional Roman Catholic methods, including the sprinkling of holy water and salt that has been blessed, and some even use old Latin prayers, though one cannot see why a spirit should know Latin rather than English if it has chosen to manifest itself in England. I personally am not convinced that these things are the effective agents, and certainly they could not be a substitute for the Name of Jesus Christ, which of course these exorcists use.

A few weeks ago a clergyman wrote to me about a case which shows how someone without previous experience was able to act simply and effectively.

In visiting a country cottage Mrs. X several times 'saw' a lady in Tudor costume, generally accompanied by a large dog with a harness collar. The lady 'told' Mrs. X that her baby, conceived by someone other than her husband, had been murdered and thrown into a well. She was distressed that it had not been baptized, and asked Mrs. X to find a priest to sprinkle holy water over the spot where the well used to be. Soon the lady began to appear to Mrs. X in her own home, although her dog did not come when Mrs. X's dog was in the room! Finally Mr. and Mrs. X felt that the matter must be resolved, and got in touch with their vicar, whom I know well. He went to their home, and, speaking about the power of the Lord Jesus Christ, told them that he did not think that holy water was the answer, but that 'only the living Christ who spanned all time could release anyone from this kind of trouble, and that we could be assured that the soul of the murdered baby has been accepted by Jesus, and covered by His work once for all on the Cross.' While he was talking, he took out his New Testament, and at this point Mrs. X 'fainted', or presumably went into a light trance. She repeated that the lady was present, and passed on to her what the vicar had said. As she came round, her tense expression had changed to one of peace, and she told her husband, 'Isn't it wonderful! She is happy now, and everything is all right'. I have since heard again that all is well.

Here is something that was dealt with quite

simply in the Name of Jesus Christ, without anyone's having to understand the way it all worked. Indeed one might discuss the case at considerable length, and still not understand it, especially if we include the dog and its harness.

More skilled advice may be needed if black magic is involved. I do not myself understand the technicalities of magic, but know there is far more to it than most people realize. Even so, Christ's victory is the defence, though the knowledge of all that is involved in the threat, haunting, or activity, is undoubtedly of extra assistance.

Some further discernment is also useful with poltergeists. Is it a person or a place that needs to be cleaned up? Does the person affect the place, or the place the person, in any one instance? If the person is the centre, is psychological help needed as well as the vital cleansing of spirit or from spirit? Nevertheless I know that 'unskilled' ministers have cleansed such poltergeistic activities in the Name of Jesus Christ.

Any Christian who is called in to help must himself be in right relationship with God. He is to take part in a spiritual operation, and must not be like a surgeon with an open wound on his hands trying to operate without gloves on a deep infection. Or, to change the picture, he cannot go into battle against an evil spirit with a large area of his life in alliance with the enemy. He first must confess his known and unknown sins, and claim the cleansing of the blood of Jesus Christ. If possible, he should have others joining in prayer either in the same room or at the same time. Prayer should be for the person, or for the driving out of the spirit or the evil from the place. The point about 'the evil' is that this may be an imprinted atmosphere from past or present.

At some point the spirit must be told in the Name of the Lord Jesus, who won the victory on the cross and rose again victoriously as the Head of every principality and power, to depart, to go to its own place, and there abide for ever. A cordon of prayer should be thrown round all present, to prevent the spirit transferring to a new host. Almost certainly this was the reason for Christ's sending of the demons into the Gadarene swine; the danger of releasing a legion of them into the crowd was very real.

To some hard-boiled readers all this will seem like fantasy, yet one day they may meet some of the phenomena we have been thinking about. When one has dismissed the fraud, the faulty observation, credulity and suggestion, that make natural happenings look like supernatural, there is enough evidence left to show that really nasty things are happening today as they have done down the ages. Science as such cannot touch them. Magic may be met by counter-magic, but only Christ can cure by conquest.

So, in closing, we must return to the reality of the Lord Jesus Christ. He was not a reincarnated man, nor a spirit being, nor a good man filled with the Spirit of God. He is true God, who became Man by genuine, though unique, conception and birth. His purpose in coming was to undo the effects of sin, to put away our guilt by bearing our sins in His sacrificial death on the cross, and to make us clean before renewing us by the inpoured life of His Spirit. Through His death and resurrection He broke the hold that Satan and his spirit followers had upon mankind, their allies. So Man can now be transferred from death to life, from the kingdom of darkness to the kingdom of God. This is the salvation and the new eternal life which begins here and now.

Yet we may still find substitutes for God's reality. Materialism invites us to 'eat and drink, for to-morrow we die', and says that death is the end. Humanism puts in a heroic claim for building up a good life here on earth, for life can have no meaning when earth and all its inhabitants have perished. Philosophy offers high thoughts for the intellectual, but refuses the light of revelation. Aestheticism rises above the physical into the sphere of inner stirrings. And, further still, there is the contact with the depths or heights of our being that may produce a mystical bliss of oneness with all life, with God still unknown, or that may bring us into contact with spirit beings whose communications lead us away from God.

Meanwhile the Christian is happy to be a material-ist, in the sense that he glorifies God in his very earthy body (1 Cor. 6. 19, 20; 2 Cor. 4. 7). He is also in a sense an unashamed humanist, since human beings are made in the likeness of God, and to be truly human in individual and social life is to be

empowered by the perfect God-Man, Jesus Christ
(Phil. 3. 8-21). He has a full pattern of sensible
philosophy which makes sense for his thinking, once
he has stepped into the Christian ring of truth
(1 Cor. 2. 6-13). He opens his aesthetic sense to the
God-given beauty of the world that keeps the sordid
at bay (Phil. 4. 8). His union with God in Christ
may or may not lead to an acute mystical awareness,
but it is union of Person with person (2 Cor. 4. 6).

Finally, in the realm of spirit contact, he sees the
whole force of the reasoning in Colossians 2. 6-23,
that, since we have union with Christ the Lord
Himself, it is not for us to use, or submit to, any
spiritual beings, whether of high or low degree.

Christians cannot retreat from this position. They
may be rebuked for their presumption in claiming
this personal link with God for the simplest and
humblest Christian. They may be told by spiritualists that they cannot expect any sudden transporta-
tion to heaven when they die, but must go on being
gradually purged and enlightened, though still without the direct vision of God. This all sounds so
natural and sensible, and Christians would never
presume to claim what they do claim if it were not
that God has promised it. The Person and work of
Jesus Christ are far wider and more glorious than
any spiritualist or occultist ever imagines.

We may well sum up with Paul's great prayer in
Ephesians 3. 14-21, which may be rendered like this:
    'I kneel in prayer to the Father, who gives
    meaning to every family relationship in heaven

and on earth, that, being gloriously rich, He
will make you strong by means of His Spirit
entering into the inner depths of your being;
that you may be linked through living trust with
Christ who has taken up His settled home in
your hearts. You will then have your root and
foundation in love. And I pray that you may
be strong enough to join all Christians in
grasping what is the breadth and length and
depth and height, i.e. to know the love of Christ
which goes far beyond human knowledge. If all
this sounds impossible I would remind you of
Him who is able to do infinitely more than we
ever ask or dream of, through the power which
is constantly at work within us. The whole
glory of the Church's life and of Christ's work
flows back to Him for ever. Amen.'